Radical Submission to God

The Awesome Life-Changing
Secret to Peace, Power & Permanent Victory!

"Submit yourselves therefore to God.
Resist the devil, and he will flee from you."
James 4:7 (KJV)

By Philip A. Matthews

Radical Submission to God
Trilogy Christian Publishers A Wholly Owned Subsidary of Trinity
Broadcasting Network
2442 Michelle Drive Tustin, CA 92780

Rights Department, 2442 Michelle Drive, Tustin, CA 92780.

Trilogy Christian Publishing/TBN and colophon are trademarks of
Trinity Broadcasting Network.

Cover design by: Natalee Dunning

For information about special discounts for bulk purchases, please
contact Trilogy Christian Publishing.

Trilogy Disclaimer: The views and content expressed in this book are
those of the author and may not necessarily reflect the views and doctrine
of Trilogy Christian Publishing or the Trinity Broadcasting Network.

Manufactured in the United States of America

10 9 8 7 6 5 4 3 2 1

Library of Congress Cataloging-in-Publication Data is available.

ISBN: 978-1-63769-944-7

E-ISBN: 978-1-63769-945-4

DEDICATION

This book is dedicated first of all to my lovely wife and partner of forty-nine years, Segatha Ruth (Douglas) Matthews, my spiritual role model, who personally taught me quite a few life lessons about submission and with whom I have been radically dedicated to God for over forty years of ministry. How she knew so much about submission, even as a young woman in her 20s, I will never know. Through seven children, a couple of periods of "living by faith" (aka full-time ministry with no real job or income!), at least forty-eight people living with us at different times, and lots of other mundane crises, she has been a rock of stability, always optimistic, always full of faith, and always happy and smiling. I have never seen her worried, losing her peace, or pulling out her hair. If she ever does, I will know then that we are in *real* trouble, the worst we have ever been in—and I will probably panic and faint!

It is also dedicated to my former pastor and mentor, the late Pastor Esau Jackson Trotter of Fresno, California, who started me on my search for a deeper discipleship and relationship with God that brings perpetual peace and joy. He was absolutely the spiritually deepest preacher I've ever known, often misunderstood because his messages were so far above the average Christian's life. I often compared him to Andrew Murray, which is saying a lot. His oft-repeated motto was, "I don't worry about *nothing*. I don't worry about a *thing!*" May he rest in peace knowing that we caught the vision.

And last of all, this book is dedicated to my Lord and Savior, Jesus Christ. I promised Him not only my own life forever but that I would do everything within my power, with the abilities He has given me, to help other people see how much God really loves them, how much trust, submission, and love they owe Him in return, and how much happiness, blessedness, and satisfaction such a mutual relationship with the Lover of our souls actually brings. Hopefully, this helps.

Philip A. Matthews
2021

ACKNOWLEDGMENTS

I would like to acknowledge the following people for their inspiration, help, and other assistance in producing this book:

- My wife, Segatha, for her endless inspiration and critical assessments. If I can say or write something that passes her tests, then it's probably decent enough to say or write.

- Our last three children to leave home, Ptolemy, Alana, and Jessieka, who were there when I first began writing this book almost two decades ago and who had to endure my constant talking about "radical submission," a topic that simply is not very interesting, comprehensible, or popular among most young people.

- My good friends, Ronald Hattley and Gloria Pierro Dyer who gave much-needed feedback, editorial notes, review questions, and other quite indispensable materials.

- My wonderful "enemies" down through my life, people, and circumstances who I will not name for discretion's sake, but without whom I would have never learned much of anything about holiness, agape love, endurance, forgiveness, spiritual healing, and so much more. I thank them immensely, for without them, I would probably still be a spiritual infant, never battle-tested, still preoccupied with ivory tower theory and theology, and still never experiencing the brokenness and crucifying necessary to gain a little of the "fellowship of His sufferings" that has made my life with Christ so satisfying and life-giving.

Thanks, one and all.

TABLE OF CONTENTS

INTRODUCTION

This little workbook is a short treatise on the theology of submission, the idea that everything in a Christian's life must be completely and radically submitted to God and subjugated to His divine will. It is relatively short—it doesn't take long to describe how to submit to God. Four little words *should* be enough: "Give it *all* up." But because we live in a religious environment where such submission is rarely practiced or seen, it has become increasingly difficult to really know what is included in that little word, "all."

We talk a lot about discipleship in today's religious world, but still, overall, the church is "seasoning" society less and less, and widespread revival is not really happening. Christians are relying more on political and social clout—voting, lobbying, protests, boycotts, court cases, email campaigns, special "God-ordained" presidents, even military might—to change the world, instead of relying on the power of God and the purity and integrity of the church.

We talk a lot about discipleship in today's religious world, but hardly anything about the *basis* of discipleship—a completely consecrated life lived *only* for God in every aspect of life. How can people truly be disciples of Christ and still have huge areas of their lives remaining under their own control?

It may be time for the church to go back and investigate the claims of the holiness movement that came out of the "Great Awakening," the Wesleyan revival, and the various subsequent, true moves of God in the 19th century. They are the theological perspectives from which this book is written. Several generations—millions of honest, sincere Christians—claimed to have experienced a radical purification from sin and self and a victory over both in their daily lives. They claimed to have totally died to themselves and that everything was completely and utterly given over to God's control. Some people today believe that this is impossible, but surely these old "holiness folks" could not *all* have been deceived. Surely there must have been at least a little merit to their claim that they were living "free from sin." Surely what they offered to the Body is worth looking at again in this age of "sinning Christians."

The Christian church, in general, was a much more powerful, more trustworthy, and more respectable institution then than it is now, where the normal Christian sins and acts selfish and worldly every day, sometimes very flagrantly and scandalously, still claiming to be saved and on their way to heaven. Sin and spiritual weakness are normal for us, expected and excused. And social opinion about us has been ruthless: Christianity today is viewed by multiple millions to be nothing but a group of selfish old hypocrites!

While reading this book, we suggest that you have a Bible handy so that when scripture references are given, you can look them up and see for yourself the passage supporting the principle or point being made. We have broken up this version of the book into small, bite-sized pieces, enabling the reader to "eat" or meditate on one section per day for forty days. Or it can be used for small group discussions for forty weeks. After each section, we have included a few questions for discussion or meditation to make the lessons more practical. Then we end with a short prayer.

Happy meditations!

Radical Submission to God:
The Awesome Life-Changing Secret to Peace, Power, and Permanent Victory

"Submit yourselves therefore to God.
Resist the devil, and he will flee from you."
James 4:7 (KJV)

CHAPTER ONE
THE ORIGINAL PROBLEM AND GOD'S SOLUTION

Lesson 1: The Original Problem and God's Solution

"All we like sheep have gone astray;
we have turned every one to his own way…"

Isaiah 53:6 (KJV)

The problem with most people is that they are rebellious to a fault. They have a problem submitting to authority—parents, teachers, employers, law enforcement officers, rules and regulations, social standards of behavior, or any other authority. But most of all, they have a problem submitting to God. Everyone wants to direct their own steps and live life the way they want to live it. Submitting to some higher authority, if done at all, is usually done with great reluctance and distaste.

We have even reached a time when most professed Christians very seldom practice, or even know much about, submission to God. What the church needs today, more than anything else, is a greater knowledge and practice of the theology of submission. This is the basis of true discipleship. It is also the secret pathway to peace, power, and permanent victory.

Back to the Beginning

Let us go back to the beginning and explain the dynamic working in all of human existence. God made man upright and obedient, but man has chosen to go his own way. "We're all like sheep who've wandered off and gotten lost. We've all done our own thing, gone our own way" (Isaiah 53:6, The Message). In the Garden, God said, "Live the way I have designed for you to live. Trust Me because I am all you will ever need." But man, prompted by Satan, chose to distrust and suspect God and disobeyed God's instructions. *That was absolute rebellion. It is the spirit behind every sin in the world since the beginning.*

Afterward, God said, "Wear this decent clothing I have designed for you, permanently cleave to the spouse I gave you, and keep all of your sexuality within your marriage, the only legitimate 'container' for human sexuality." Humans, in rebellion, have said, "I will wear whatever I want to wear and flaunt my sexuality. I will marry whoever I want to marry and as many times as I want to marry." Or, "I will skip marriage altogether and spread my sexuality all over the place—if I want to."

Time went on. Then God said, "As your Creator, I want you to worship me in a certain way with which I am well pleased. Here are the specifications." Some men, such as Abel, followed God's instructions. But others, like Cain, came up with their own way to worship God, rebelliously trying to force Him to be well pleased with it anyway. God demanded to be worshiped as the only God because He is, but human beings have always worshiped other things and other spirits as god.

Later, God said, "Don't steal. Don't lie. Be satisfied; don't covet." But we have rebelled and refused to be satisfied. Greed and unrestrained desire are rebellion. So then, we are forced to lie and steal and cheat. God said, Be humble by acknowledging that I am the only source of life, goodness, blessings, and peace. Instead, we have chosen to be proud, egotistically acting as if we ourselves are gods and have the ability, independent of God, to produce blessings and goodness. So, pride and ego are rebellion.

As time went on, God gave more instructions: "Believe in Me; believe in My Son. Believe in My love." But we have chosen to remain in unbelief, which is rebellion. Trust in Me, He says. But we have chosen, in rebellion, to worry and stress ourselves to death, to put our trust in things that ultimately do not and cannot help us or bring us peace. We have chosen to remain in fear and allow our lives to be ruled by it. *Fear is rebellion.*

And for those who don't believe that fear and unbelief are serious forms of rebellion, listen to Jesus in Revelation 21:8 (KJV), where fear and unbelief are first in the list of sins: "But the fearful, and unbelieving, and the abominable, and murderers, and whoremongers, and sorcerers, and idolaters, and all liars, shall have their part in the lake which burneth with fire and brimstone: which is the second death." Rebellion is bad stuff!

QUESTIONS:

1. What is the original problem that all people are born with?
2. How have you seen rebellion manifested in your own life?
3. What do you think is the solution to this problem?

PRAYER:

Oh, heavenly Father, we acknowledge that "we're all like sheep who've wandered off and gotten lost. We've all done our own thing, gone our own way" (Isaiah 53:6, The Message). For this, we confess and ask Your continual forgiveness. Help us to hear You and be willing to follow You. In Jesus' name, amen.

Lesson 2: Rebellion Underlies Every Form of Sin

"Behold, this only have I found: that God has made man upright, but they have sought out many perversions."

Ecclesiastes 7:29 (Jubilee Bible)

Look at the following New Testament lists of common human behaviors and notice how the spirit of rebellion is behind each behavior listed in these catalogs of sin. Notice how each sin is characterized by a blatant refusal to be controlled by the moral laws of God, the law of conscience, reason or common sense, the expectations of society, or even the rules of nature. They demonstrate people's absolute refusal to allow their personal desires and drives to be limited in any form or fashion by anything:

- *Romans 1:25–32 (KJV):* "Who changed the truth of God into a lie, and worshipped and served the creature more than the Creator, who is blessed forever. Amen. For this cause God gave them up unto vile affections: for even their women did change the natural use into that which is against nature: and likewise also the men, leaving the natural use of the woman, burned in their lust one toward another; men with men working that which is unseemly, and receiving in themselves that recompense of their error which was meet. And even as they did not like to retain God in their knowledge, God gave them over to a reprobate mind, to do those things which are not convenient ["proper or decent"—AMP]; being filled with all unrighteousness, fornication, wickedness, covetousness, maliciousness; full of envy, murder, debate, deceit, malignity; whisperers, backbiters, haters of God, despiteful, proud, boasters, inventors of evil things, disobedient to parents, without understanding, covenant-breakers, without natural affection, implacable, unmerciful: who knowing the judgment of God, that they which commit such things are worthy of death, not only do the same, but have pleasure in them that do them."

- *First Corinthians 6:9–11 (KJV):* "Know ye not that the unrighteous shall not inherit the kingdom of God? Be not deceived: neither fornicators, nor idolaters, nor adulterers, nor effeminate, nor abusers of themselves with mankind, nor thieves, nor covetous, nor drunkards, nor revilers, nor extortioners, shall inherit the kingdom of God. And such were some of you: but ye are washed, but ye are sanctified, but ye are justified in the name of the Lord Jesus, and by the Spirit of our God."

- *Second Timothy 3:1–5 (AMP):* "But understand this, that in the last days will come (set in) perilous times of great stress and trouble [hard to deal with and hard to bear]. For people will be lovers of self and [utterly] self-centered, lovers of money and aroused by an inordinate [greedy] desire for wealth, proud and arrogant and contemptuous boasters. They will be abusive (blasphemous, scoffing), disobedient to parents, ungrateful, unholy and profane. [They will be] without natural [human] affection (callous and inhuman), relentless (admitting of no truce or appeasement); [they will be] slanderers (false accusers, troublemakers), intemperate and loose in morals and conduct, uncontrolled and fierce, haters of good. [They will be] treacherous [betrayers], rash, [and] inflated with self-conceit. [They will be] lovers of sensual pleasures and vain amusements more than and rather than lovers of God. For [although] they hold a form of piety (true religion), they deny and reject and are strangers to the power of it [their conduct belies the genuineness of their profession]. Avoid [all] such people [turn away from them]."

- *Revelation 21:8 (KJV):* "But the fearful, and unbelieving, and the abominable, and murderers, and whoremongers, and sorcerers, and idolaters, and all liars, shall have their part in the lake which burns with fire and brimstone: which is the second death."

Thus, rebellion, in its various forms, is the chief spirit working in the world, from the Beginning until now. *It is actually the only sin in the world!* Obviously, in order to save the world, the first thing that must be dealt with is this damnable spirit of rebellion. Conquer that, and the whole world could be saved. Overcome rebellion and peace in every facet of human life could exist. But fail to deal with rebellion, and everything is hopelessly hellish.

So that is why God sent Jesus, in the form of an obedient servant of God, to teach us submission—the opposite of rebellion. *This is God's solution to the universal problem.* Jesus is submission and humility personified. *He, Submission, is the only way to life.* Read John 14:6 in this new light: "I, Submission Personified, Am the Way, the Truth, and the Life." So, once we learn submission, we will have solved the chief problem in the world—or at least in your own individual life.

QUESTIONS:

1. Review at least five of the human behaviors listed in the scriptures above and identify which of the laws of God or morality it is rebelling against.
2. Explain how the new reading of John 14:6 is true.

PRAYER:

Blessed Lord, help us to see the depth of rebellion in all natural human behavior. Help us to discern then reject such behavior in our own lives. Help us not to have only an *"outward form of piety but deny its power to change our lives."* And lead us in the *"way everlasting,"* i.e., *"that leads to true eternal life."* In the name of our Savior, amen.

Lesson 3: God's Plan of Salvation through Radical Submission

"God was in Christ, reconciling the world unto Himself, not imputing their trespasses unto them; and hath committed unto us the word of reconciliation."

2 Corinthians 5:19 (KJV)

In the beginning, God made a "hybrid" creature called human beings, a combination of animal/physical and angel/spiritual, able to commune with Him on the spiritual level but also part of the physical world. Man is thus an in-between creature, unique in this world. As the Psalmist asked, "What is man that thou art mindful of him? and the son of man that thou visitest him? For thou hast made him a little lower than the angels, and hast crowned him with glory & honor" (Psalm 8:4–5, KJV).

All of the love God had ("God *is* love;" it is not from the earth but from outside of this world) flowed freely between Him and His new human creation. All of heaven's blessings flowed freely into man's life. The result was that people were blessed and secure. They knew that they were valued and esteemed. They knew their identity and significance, purpose, reason for living, and the meaning of life. There was no worry or anxiety, nothing to be afraid of or even threatened by. In fact, they had no real knowledge that threats even existed because they had not yet eaten from the Tree of the Knowledge of Good and Evil. But then, how could they *not* have such an ideal existence when all of the love and blessings of heaven were flowing freely to them through the spiritual channel/ connection they had with God?

Then they rebelled and disobeyed, and that connection was severed. The love, blessings, and spiritual communion ceased. This left them without a direct connection to His love and all of the above benefits. Without this spiritual connection, they fell completely under the power of their physical dimension alone. They immediately felt *fear*, which is the *natural result* of being disconnected from God and security. *Without love flowing, fear rules.* People are now born into fear automatically. Adam and Eve also immediately felt guilt, which is a form of spiritual fear and insecurity.

Almost every negative thing we feel is merely a form of this fear: insecurity, low self-esteem, feelings of worthlessness and insignificance, lost identity, purposelessness, worry, anxiety, unprotected-ness, aloneness, permanent anger, pride, hatred, bitterness, resentment, jealousy, unforgiveness, unthankfulness, cynicism, dissatisfaction, lack of peace, blaming God, being controlling, being driven by what others think, craving approval and acceptance, hiding behind facades and putting up fronts, impatience, perfectionism, timidity, depression, feelings of abandonment, contentiousness, aggressiveness, and dozens more.

Most human actions and behavior are merely a response and adaptation to cope with this fear and substitute something for the love we are now missing from God:

- Acting selfishly;
- Obsession with survival ("self-preservation is the first law of nature");
- Oversensitivity (to stay on the alert for any real or imagined threats);

- Hoarding of anything gained (power, money, fame, opportunities, or anything considered valuable, to build a hedge of protection and security around oneself);
- All the forms of aggressiveness and fighting (to bluff and scare others off, to keep them from taking advantage of you, to get revenge, to teach them a lesson, etc.);
- Drinking, drugging, sexual carousing, and pleasure-seeking (to anesthetize oneself to the fear and pain of living separated from God by altering one's *perception* of reality);
- The obsession with seeking significance, fame, attention, immortality through great building projects, educational attainments, entertainment, etc.;
- Constant preoccupation with external appearance (billions spent on "beauty" products and procedures);
- Busyness/being a workaholic; being a control freak;
- Aloofness (withholding emotions from others, even family, to avoid getting hurt again);
- Difficulties in maintaining relationships, etc.

This should give us a new perspective on how God looks at sin. To us, we believe people are just being sinful because they are evil and just want to be wicked. We see ourselves as being evil, sometimes so evil we wonder if God would ever forgive us, and we definitely have a problem forgiving ourselves. But God, on the other hand, sees sin merely as the natural, automatic "*Symptoms of Disconnectedness.*" What else *can* we do? How else *can* we act? Without His love flowing into and through us, how can we act/react otherwise? Psalm 103:13–14 (NKJV): "As a Father pities His children, so the Lord pities those who fear Him. For He knows our frame (Hebrew *yetser*, i.e., our formation, the manner in which we are constructed, i.e., a "hybrid," and the materials of which we are made [body and spirit]). "He remembers that we are dust," i.e., under the power of our dust-formed, physical bodies.

God has compassion and mercy on us because He knows we cannot do anything *except* act like orphans cut off from love and every positive hope in the world—because we *are*. He is thus much more ready to forgive our sins when they are viewed as "symptoms of disconnectedness." We don't have an excuse, but there *is* a reason why we sin.

So then, we are spiritual beings now trapped in an all-physical world. Even though many people live like animals, in touch with and indulging only their physical dimension, we still have spiritual longings, a need to have meaning in our lives, a desire to make our lives count for something, a fear that we are alone in the universe, etc., stuff that no mere animal or dog ever feels. These desires have made every society in history a very religious society, seeking to worship something though few have really known *who* or *what* to worship.

But unless God reaches down to us, there is absolutely no way we would ever get out of this trap. Now, why would He reach down? Because, since He is love by definition, He is bound to *not* abandon His souls/spiritual beings trapped in this physical realm. His very essence *requires* Him to do something, and what He needs to do is somehow to interject some of that missing love back into this world by reconnecting them to Himself. Being reconnected to the Source of all love and heavenly blessedness would literally *revolutionize* our lives!

Thus, God Himself, as love, absolutely *must* come down into our realm. Hence, "For God so loved the world, that He gave His only begotten Son, that whosoever believes in Him might not perish but have everlasting life" (John 3:16, KJV). This is the greatest, most profound verse in the Bible!

The first thing God, in the form of Jesus Christ, had to do was to atone for and remove our sins, which was what prevented us from being connected to Him in the first place. Next, He had to usher in the Holy Spirit, which is how God actually flows in and through our spiritual dimension once we are reconnected. He also had to personally demonstrate to us how, as human beings, we have to deny and crucify, i.e., *submit,* our human selves and fleshly lives on a "cross" in order to permit God's Spirit to be able *to continue* to flow in us. Submission of our will and our ways allows this whole plan of salvation to work for us. Then He went on back to heaven.

This process is God's plan of salvation in a nutshell. The whole thing is about reconnection, or, in the words of the Apostle Paul in 2 Corinthians 5:17–21 (KJV), *reconciliation:*

> Therefore if any man be in Christ, he is a new creature: old things are passed away; behold, all things are become new. And all things are of God, who hath reconciled us to himself by Jesus Christ, and hath given to us the *ministry of reconciliation*; To (summarize): *That God was in Christ, reconciling the world unto Himself, not imputing their trespasses unto them; and hath committed unto us the word of reconciliation.* Now then we are ambassadors for Christ, as though God did beseech you by us: we pray you in Christ's stead, *be ye reconciled* to God. For he hath made him to be sin for us, who knew no sin; that we might be made the righteousness of God in him.

Once we are reconnected to God and His love and Spirit are freely flowing into and through us, the ideal result is that all fear in its every form evaporates. No worry or anxiety. No being driven to act out in selfish ways. All love, "righteousness, peace, and joy in the Holy Spirit" (Romans 14:17, KJV). The Apostle John says that "There is no fear in love; but perfect love casts out FEAR… He that fears is not made perfect in love" (1 John 4:18, KJV).

So, if only 10 percent of Christians ever experience this victory over all fear, what is happening to the remaining 90 percent of them? Why are they still acting like orphans? *They are allowing their human self-lives to dam up the flow of love from heaven.* Some, unfortunately, have never experienced God pouring His awesome love out into their lives (Romans 5:5) and thus need to pray for that experience. Others are refusing or neglecting to empty themselves and live under submission, which is what Jesus Christ came to show us how and empower us to do. They are refusing to receive the Spirit or to walk in the Spirit so that they "do not fulfill the desires of the flesh" (Galatians 5:16–18, KJV). The patterns of thinking and acting which are learned while disconnected must be changed by the power of the Holy Spirit through one's daily disciplines. "And be constantly renewed in the spirit of your mind [having a fresh mental and spiritual attitude]" (Ephesians 4:23, AMP). This ongoing process of emptying oneself is called "sanctification," and radical submission is what makes the transformation possible.

In short, rebellion plunged the world into the icy, deathly cold ocean of sin, and ingrained rebellion has kept us submerged and drowning there. Surrender restores, and ongoing submission maintains our spiritual connection to God's Spirit and the in-finite blessings He bestows on us. That is, submission brings us life again. *And the quality of that life depends on the degree of our submission to God.*

1. How does it make you feel when you realize that all of your sins and struggles with evil have been nothing more than "symptoms of disconnectedness?"
2. Have you experienced a personal deliverance from fear?

PRAYER:

Lord, we thank You so much for Your love that enables us to be reconciled to You! Without being connected, we know that we are utterly lost. But millions, Lord, are not aware of this truth. Please work in us in such a way that it will be obvious to all that we are connected to God Almighty so that others will want this too. Use us, like You used Paul in his "ministry of reconciliation," to bring souls to You. Amen.

Lesson 4: Orphans Versus King's Kids

"For [if we are] in Christ Jesus, neither circumcision nor uncircumcision counts for anything, but only faith activated and energized and expressed and working through love."

Galatians 5:6 (AMP)

Now it should be noted that the reason and motivation for us being able to truly submit to God is that we *experientially know* He loves us completely, profoundly, and unconditionally. Otherwise, it makes absolutely no sense for us to submit our very existence into the hands and control of some invisible being, a being that most people only believe is imaginary and, at best, fickle and arbitrary. We absolutely *must* know, by divine revelation and experiential knowledge, with our hearts and not merely our heads that God loves us *totally*. We must *experience* His love fully. Then we can trust Him fully. In other words, faith is produced by love.

So radical submission, denying and dying to self, absolute surrender, etc., are all to be *responses* to the love you are receiving, on an ongoing basis, from the Father. Receiving His love *enables* you to submit to Him. And the more of His great, marvelous, life-changing love you receive and feel, the more completely you will be able to submit to Him and let Him have absolute control of your entire life.

Radical submission is enabled because you have radical faith and trust in God's radical love for you. You become willing to submit *only after* you realize just how great is the Father's love for you. If this were a chemical formula or something, it would look like this:

Radical Love → Radical Faith/Trust → Radical Submission

If you know by revelation and experience that He unconditionally loves you, then you will definitely be able to trust Him with everything. Total faith is the basis for total submission. You simply cannot submit if you do not believe, and you cannot believe if you don't feel His love. This is how "faith works (is activated and energized) by love."

Intimate knowledge of His love will give you confidence, where there was once insecurity and low self-esteem; peace, where there was once fear, worry, and anxiety; and the ability to let that love overflow onto others, where there was once the tendency to think only all about yourself. As a *totally loved* person, I can help you find yours because I've already got mine.

So, this is all about a relationship—with the almighty, all-loving, all-knowing God of the universe. For some reason, He loves you, unworthy and pitiful creature that you are. All He wants is for you to love Him in return—by giving Him your life and releasing everything into His loving hands. But you are more than glad to do this because your life is totally safe in His love—*when you experience it.*

Now, what are the ramifications of such a relationship? It's the profound difference between being, on the one hand, a scared little orphan, having no one to love him, to protect him, and to be the strength of his life, or, on the other hand, a well-kept, very-loved, special child of a King.

An orphan feels like he has to fight for survival. He's sensitive, always on guard, so no one takes advantage of his lack of having a protector. He's naturally anxious and worried that the worse will always happen. He lives in fear. Fear rules his life, influencing every decision he makes, every thought he thinks, every attitude he adopts, every action he takes. He's got only himself to take care of himself, an extremely precarious predicament!

By contrast, the well-kept, very-loved King's kid can relax. No need to worry; Daddy will take care of *everything*. So what if circumstances look bad? I've got my Father inside of me, and He's all I need. I don't miss the *gift* because I possess the *Giver*. People might think I'm nothing, but so what? My Father thinks I'm "the bomb." *My great value comes from the love He's placed on me.* Don't know why He values me so much, but that's just how He is. You hate me? Well, guess what? *He* loves me. So that makes me able to completely disregard your hatred. Even better—it makes me able to return *love* to you for your hatred.

There Is a King In You
By Donald Lawrence
http://www.youtube.com/watch?v=jTq0EmSr5gE&feature=player_embedded

You come from royalty
An aristocratic dynasty
The goal of the enemy
Is that you don't know who you are
There's power when you speak
Be mindful of words you release
Is there no King in you, then why do you speak
Speak with such defeat?
Is there no King in you, then why do you speak
Speak with such low esteem?
I know that life has challenged you
But the King in me speaks to the King in you
You were born to rule, there is a King in you

QUESTIONS:

1. Would you agree that the most important thing for a person to grasp and experience is how great the Father's love is for him/her personally? Why?
2. Have you experienced that great love personally, or would you say that you still sometimes doubt it?

PRAYER:

Father God, Daddy, Lover of our souls, thank You for adopting us, weak, puny, sinful, very unworthy, and embarrassing, into Your family of All-Stars! Now that we feel Your great, eternal love for us, we have everything we need forever, with absolutely *nothing* to worry about! *The orphaned pauper life is over forever!* Help us to live daily as well-kept, very loved King's kids. Keep us always aware of our permanent status in You. In the name of our Big Brother, Jesus Christ, amen.

Lesson 5: The Supreme Substitute

"The LORD is my shepherd; I have everything I need."

Psalm 23:1 (Good News Bible)

Since I am so deeply aware that God loves me so totally, *I don't need anything else* to make my existence blessed and my heart happy. My blessedness doesn't depend on anything, anybody, or any set of circumstances *outside of Him.* I am truly beyond the reach of trouble.

He has become the supreme substitute for all of the trivialities we human beings long for and cling to trying to find happiness, fulfillment, purpose, and meaning in life. He satisfies better than a great financial success, which is still transient at its best. He is sweeter than a wonderful husband or that wonder-woman trophy wife. That husband is still just a man, and no man is perfect. So, during his time of imperfection (no matter how troublesome they might be), I still have the steady love that comes only from Jesus, the true Lover of my soul. In essence, then, *Jesus* is the perfect husband, and I can let that little guy "with skin on" off the hook when he fails. Don't even expect to get everything you really need from even the best man. Only God can do that.

I Will Glory

Verse 1:
I'm not looking for this world to favor me,
For my strength is coming from the Lord above.
I can't count on circumstances, Don't depend on luck or chances.
Jesus, I am trusting only in Your love.

Chorus:
So I will glory... I'll glory in Jesus...
Lord, I lift my heart and hands to You alone.
In the midst of tribulation, In the valley of temptation,
I will glory in the One Who died for me.

Verse 2:
Jesus, You're my Joy and Source of happiness.
And there's nothing like Your love I must confess.
And there is nothing like the peace
You so freely give to me!
Your amazing grace has made my life so blessed!

Verse 3:
You have lifted me above the howling storm.
You have placed my life beyond the reach of harm.
You have taken all my fears, You have wiped away my tears.
So I will glory in the One Who sets me free.

Ending:
All is well, all is well, All is well with my soul, all is well...
[© 2006 by Philip Matthews]

So, God, the Father, Jesus, the Son, and the Holy Spirit, the "Comforter," are the perfect, Supreme Substitute for everything we wish we had and die struggling to obtain: perfect circumstances, perfect friends, perfect marriages, trouble-free days, enviable financial blessings, etc., etc., etc. If we really know and fully feel God's love, all these other little things become almost dispensable. And we remain happy and unworried, steady and anchored, not tossed into turmoil and despair by the bad stuff or raised up to unstable emotional heights by the good, in a tiresome yo-yo fashion.

Two more verses of song immediately come to mind: the old hymn by Henry F. Lyte:

Jesus, I My Cross Have Taken

Jesus, I my cross have taken, All to leave and follow Thee;
Naked, poor, despised, forsaken, Thou, from hence, my all shalt be.
Perish every fond ambition, All I've sought, or hoped or known,
Yet how rich is my condition! God and heaven are still my own…

Man may trouble and distress me. 'Twill but drive me to Thy breast.
Life with trials hard may press me. Heaven will bring me sweeter rest.
Oh, 'tis not in grief to harm me, While Thy love is left to me.
Oh, 'twere not in joy to charm me, Were that joy unmixed with Thee.

And then, another one of my own songs, "Lead Me Safely Home" (from The Matthews Family, *Original Worship*, 2012, https://www.youtube.com/watch?v=s44gQXdhKQw. Purchase at https://www.amazon.com/Lead-Me-Safely-Home/dp/B008PVJ59S):

Jesus, I surrender My all into Your hands.
And, Jesus, I will trust You, and fit into Your plans.
Let me feel Your presence, and all Your glory know.
Just use me for Your pleasure, then lead me safely home.

With Your grace to guide me, With Your hand to hide me,
With Your peace inside me, I can carry on.
So, Jesus, I'm depending on Your love alone.
So take me, Lord, and hold me, and lead me safely home.

The truth of the matter is that too many Christians are seeking daily for something or somebody to satisfy their souls when they already have free access to the Supreme Substitute—God's perfect love. Very, very few of them ever find this degree of satisfaction in God.

But *you* can. Relax and let go. *Choose* to be satisfied and content. "Godliness accompanied with contentment... is great and abundant gain" (1 Timothy 6:6, AMP). "I have learned," the Apostle Paul wrote, "how to be content (satisfied to the point where I am not disturbed or disquieted) in whatever state I am in" (Philippians 4:11, AMP). *Since the beginning in the Garden, dissatisfaction has always been the motivation or catalyst for every sinful behavior. So will to be satisfied.*

As St. Augustine of Hippo said, "Desire only God and your heart will be satisfied." Set your will to forgive and forget. You've got God's powerful love on your side! No need to keep fighting and struggling. Keep this attitude of heart and mind, even if you have to reaffirm it twenty times a day. *Submit to the God who loves you with a powerful, unfailing, perfect love.* Resist the devil, and he and all the misery he has caused you will flee.

QUESTIONS:

1. The Apostles, New Testament authors, old and modern-day songwriters, and Christians since ancient times have all written that God is all we'll ever need. Jesus alone is enough. How literal is this to be taken? Or is this only theory and theology?
2. Explain and meditate on the truth found in St Augustine's quote, "Desire only God and your heart will be satisfied." Connect it to Psalm 37:4.

PRAYER:

O Lord, it is one thing to state that "You are *all* we need," but something much more difficult to actually *live* like You are indeed everything we need. Please help us to actually believe this so firmly that we can stake our lives on this. Help us to find this special river of life. And help us to put this profound secret into daily practice. In the name of our Divine Satisfier, amen.

Lesson 6: Quotes on the Relationship between Love, Faith, and Submission

"How excellent is thy lovingkindness ["steadfast love"—AMP], O God! therefore the children of men put their trust under the shadow of thy wings."

Psalm 36:7 (KJV)

Following are several profound statements regarding the relationship between faith and submission, quoted here for contemplation and discussion:

"Either we are adrift in chaos or we are individuals, created, loved, upheld and placed purposefully, exactly where we are.
Can you believe that?
Can you trust God for that?"
Elisabeth Elliot, missionary and wife of Jim Elliot, who, along with four other men were killed by the wild Huaorani tribe of Ecuador.

"God always gives His best to those who leave the choice with Him."
Jim Elliot, missionary to South America, who along with four other men was killed by the wild Huaorani tribe of Ecuador.

"Since God offers to manage our affairs for us, let us once and for all hand them over to His infinite wisdom in order to occupy ourselves
only with Himself and what belongs to Him."
Jean Pierre de Caussade, a French Jesuit priest and writer, known for his work *Abandonment to Divine Providence* (also

translated as *The Sacrament of the Present Moment*) and his work with Nuns of the Visitation in Nancy, France.

"The will of God for your life is simply that you submit yourself to Him each day and say, 'Father, Your will for today is mine. Your pleasure for today is mine. Your work for today is mine. I trust You to be God.
You lead me today and I will follow.'"
Kay Arthur, international Bible teacher, four-time ECPA Christian Book Award-winning author, and co-CEO of Precept Ministries International.

"Accept as good whatever happens to you or affects you, knowing that nothing happens without God."
The Didache (or *The Teaching of the Twelve Apostles*) is a brief early Christian treatise, dated by most scholars to the late 1st or 2nd century but not included in the New Testament canon.

"The opposite of joy is not sorrow. It is unbelief."
Leslie Weatherhead, an English theologian in the liberal Protestant tradition,
author of *The Will of God*.

"Inside the will of God there is no failure.
Outside the will of God there is no success."
Bernard Edinger, a French Jewish journalist who grew up in New York, worked in Israel, and now lives in Paris.

"God governs in the affairs of men. And if a sparrow cannot fall to the ground without His notice, is it probable that an empire can rise without His aid?"
Benjamin Franklin, an original American Founding Father.

"You never know how much you believe anything until its truth or falsehood becomes a matter of life and death to you."

C. S. Lewis, novelist, poet, academic, literary critic, essayist, lay theologian, Christian apologist, and former atheist

"God is so big He can cover the whole world with His Love and so small He can curl up inside your heart."
June Masters Bacher, author of many Christian romances, the most popular being *Love is a Gentle Stranger*.

Living by Faith

By James Wells / J. L. Heath

Verse 1:

I care not today what the morrow may bring, if shadow or sunshine or rain,
The Lord I know rules over everything, and all of my worries are vain

Chorus:

Living by faith in Jesus alone, Trusting, confiding in His great Love.
From all harm safe, in His sheltering arm, I'm living by faith and feel no alarm.

Verse 2:

Though tempests may blow and the storm clouds arise, obscuring the brightness of life,
I'm never alarmed at the overcast skies, the Master looks on at the strife.

Verse 3:

I know that He safely will carry me through, no matter what evils betide.
Why should I then care, though the tempest may blow, if Jesus walks close to my side?

QUESTIONS:

1. Is it even humanly possible to do as the songwriter wrote: "I care not today what the morrow may bring"? Is it really possible not to care about the future?
2. What would be the results of such an attitude of complete trust?

PRAYER:

Oh, heavenly Father, we can see on paper that trusting You brings the most blessedness a human being can experience. But, Lord, trusting You is also one of the most difficult things for a human being to do. So, we pray today that You will give us a greater revelation of Your awesome, incredible love for each of us individually so that it will be easier for us to trust You and have faith to believe in You and submit to You. This earnest prayer we pray in the name of the One Who loves us with an infinite, everlasting love, Jesus Christ, amen.

CHAPTER TWO
HOW TO PRACTICE RADICAL SUBMISSION

Lesson 7: How Is Submission Defined?

"Submit yourselves therefore to God. Resist the devil, and he will flee from you."

James 4:7 (KJV)

The word translated "submission" in James 4:7 is actually the Greek word *hupotasso*, meaning to subject or place oneself under. It is a combination of *hupo* meaning "under" and *tasso* meaning "to arrange." According to *Vine's Expository Dictionary of Old and New Testament Words*, it is primarily a military term, meaning to "rank under," i.e., to subject oneself, to obey, to be subject to. The genealogy of the word means "to arrange oneself under or to array oneself with." Thus, when James says to "submit to God," he is instructing us *to arrange everything in our lives under and to array ourselves with the Will, the Word, and the Spirit of God.*

What is significant is that he continues with the instructions, "resist the devil." This word, "resist," is from the Greek word *anthistemi*, meaning "to cause to stand against; to array oneself against." Thus, it is the opposite of the phrase, "to submit." So then the complete instructions are to array ourselves *with* God so that we can array ourselves *against* the devil. And here is the truth on which these instructions are based: *One cannot success-*

fully resist the devil unless and until *he has arranged himself and everything in his life under God. Everything in his life that is not brought under subjection to God is automatically vulnerable and susceptible to the devil.*

This is a very important concept. Too many Christians go around trying to resist the devil, trying to keep him out of their lives, when they have never arranged their lives completely under God. That is, they have never completely submitted to God. By submitting everything in their lives to God, they place themselves squarely on His territory and in His impenetrable divine protection.

God is holy, meaning, among other things, that He is infinitely above and completely separated from the corrupt mess of the world of normal humanity. By perfectly submitting ourselves to God and bringing *everything* in our lives under Him, we attach ourselves to God's holiness and separateness and are thereby lifted above the normal human condition. In that condition of perfect submission, absolutely nothing in life—"good" things or "bad" things—can ever really harm us. But by failing or neglecting to arrange ourselves completely under God, we remain vulnerable and in danger, on the devil's territory, where he can cause us permanent damage and misery.

QUESTIONS:

1. Is everything in your life completely "arranged under God?" Is it all under God, or are there some things sticking out? Are there any areas of your life that you yourself are operating in your own way? Write these down so that you can think about what you are going to do about this situation.

PRAYER:

Lord, help us to be willing to "arrange everything" under Your command and control. Show us the areas of our lives where we ourselves are still running the show. In Jesus' name, we pray, amen.

Lesson 8: Submission Is Learned Through the Cross

"Jesus is God's own Son, but still He had to suffer before He could learn what it really means to obey God."

Hebrews 5:8 (CEV)

God is omniscient, knowing all things, but there is one thing that God in the flesh had to learn: how to submit, as a human being, to the will and way of the Father. "Though He were a Son [i.e., a human being] .... Yet learned He obedience [submission] by the things which He suffered" (Hebrews 5:8, KJV).

This is an incredibly significant concept, one of the greatest in the Bible and the most important in the world for us human beings. Jesus Christ was God in the flesh, a wonderful worker of miracles, Teacher of world-shaking truth, Giver of life to the dead, and so forth. But as a man, He had to *learn* the lesson that is actually the secret to all life: *The way to life is obtained and maintained by completely submitting to God.* True life is found *only* in God—His Being, His Way, His Word, His Spirit. Thus, only by attaching ourselves to God through submission to Him can we experience real life.

This "suffering" that Jesus underwent was actually more than His physical suffering. Remember, it was in the Garden of Gethsemane before He had even been arrested, while He still wrestled with His humanity to submit to the will of God, that He went through His greatest suffering. It is only when something hurts or displeases our flesh or crosses our own preferences and desires that we can say that we are "suffering." And it is when we suffer that we are tempted to forsake God's way and take our own.

It is easy to go God's way when His way coincides with our own. It is easy to choose His will when our desires match His. But it is extremely difficult to cooperate with Him when His desires for us cross our own desires for ourselves.

In fact, that is the spiritual definition of the "cross:" When *His* way "crosses" *our* way. It is only when His way crosses ours, but we choose His way *anyway* that we are actually "taking up our cross" and denying ourselves. Matthew 16:24 (KJV): "If any man will come after me, let him deny himself, and take up his cross, and follow me." It is only at those times that we are really practicing obedience and submission.

Many of today's Christians have forgotten that the cross is the crux of the matter in Christianity. *A cross-less Christianity is not Christianity at all!* Worship, praise, feeling the Spirit, and Bible knowledge are all wonderful and necessary elements of the faith, but let us not forget that the cross is what makes a Christian: *only perfect submission to the will of God.*

The cross is what makes a true disciple of Christ, as defined by Jesus Himself: "If you want to be my follower you must love me more than [Greek 'you must hate or love less'] your own father and mother, wife and children, brothers and sisters—yes, more than your own life. Otherwise, you cannot be my disciple. And you cannot be my disciple if you do not carry your own cross and follow me" (Luke 14:26–27, NLT).

When we insist on trying to be a Christian without "hating" our own lives, without bearing our crosses, and without completely subjugating our own will, wishes, and whims under God, then we are trying to do something that Jesus Christ Himself has already told us is impossible. You *cannot* keep doing your own thing and still be His disciple. *Case closed.*

QUESTIONS:

1. What is the spiritual definition of the "cross" that Jesus speaks about?
2. In what way did I choose to "take up my cross" recently by choosing God's way instead of my own?

PRAYER:

Heavenly Father, help me take up my cross daily and follow You. In Your name, amen.

Lesson 9: Step One to Submission:
Make a Complete Consecration

*"I beseech you therefore, brethren, by the mercies of God, that ye
present your bodies a living sacrifice, holy, acceptable unto God..."*

Romans 12:1a (KJV)

This is how to practice submission to God in your everyday life.
*First of all, you must initially yield your will to God in a complete
consecration.* Once and for all, give God your whole life and everything in it:

- Everything you now are, and everything you hope to be;
- All your plans, dreams, and personal ambitions;
- All your opportunities; all your reputation and image;
- All your desires and preferences;
- All your standards and demands of what your life must
  become or not become;
- All your habits of behavior;
- All your possessions, including all your money;
- All your rights and privileges to do, go, say, or think
  whatever you want;
- All your relationships and associations, including your
  romantic involvements and your total sexuality;
- All your rights to obligate yourself, your time, your strength,
  your emotions, and your money;

- Your power to make decisions without first consulting the Lord;
- And everything else (if anything is still left!).

In addition, *You must relinquish up to Him your rights to demand that other people treat you right and that they recognize and respect you like you want them to.* You must relinquish up to Him the privilege to *not* forgive other people, to hold on to resentment and hurt feelings, to exact revenge—all of this you place in the hands of God. You must give up your right to sin and to live selfishly. You must give Him everything that makes you, you. *Your whole life!*

You must give Him your life as a blank check on which He can write any demands and require any personal sacrifices. He must have the sole say-so in your life from now on. You reserve absolutely no rights and privileges to your own self. You hold back nothing. God owns all of that now. You don't own anything!

In religious terms, we liken this consecration process to "absolute surrender" (Andrew Murray), "sanctification" (Wesley and the holiness movement), or "placing yourself on the altar" as a "living sacrifice" to God (the Apostle Paul): "So here's what I want you to do, God helping you: Take your everyday, ordinary life—your sleeping, eating, going-to-work, and walking-around life—and place it before God as an offering…" (Romans 12:1, The Message).

A sacrifice or offering is at the disposal of the one to whom it is sacrificed. A sacrifice does not have its own plans. A sacrifice doesn't live by its own dreams and ambitions. A sacrifice *dies.* A sacrifice does not jump up off the altar because the fire is too hot and demands to have its own way. A sacrifice does not say, "Enough is enough! I'll give *this* much, but *that* much is just absolutely *too* much!" A sacrifice has no say in what it is going to be used for.

What happens to the sacrifice is determined solely by the one to whom it is sacrificed—in this case, God.

Take Jesus as the example of a perfect sacrifice. He was completely yielded and under subjection to His Father, even when it meant He had to die, *to be literally disposed of.*

This is complete consecration, according to Frances R. Havergal, one of the most dedicated Christian women of the 19th century, in her famous hymn:

Take My Life and Let It Be

Take my life and let it be Consecrated, Lord, to Thee.
Take my hands and let them move At the impulse of Thy love.

Take my feet and let them be Swift and beautiful for Thee.
Take my voice and let me sing, Always, only for my King.

Take my lips and let them be Filled with messages from Thee.
Take my silver and my gold, Not a mite would I withhold.

Take my moments and my days, Let them flow in endless praise.
Take my intellect and use Every pow'r as Thou shalt choose.

Take my will and make it Thine, It shall be no longer mine.
Take my heart, it is Thine own, It shall be Thy royal throne.

Take my love, my Lord, I pour At Thy feet its treasure store.
Take myself and I will be Ever, only, all for Thee.

QUESTIONS:

1. Which of the consecrations listed above is the hardest to give up to God?
2. Is the idea of being a "sacrifice" too radical?
3. Take time now to name the person(s) whom you wish would begin to treat you right.

   Take your resentment, hurt feelings, and deepest wishes about them and ask God this: "Will You take over these situations now and help me to forgive them?"

PRAYER:

Oh, Jesus, we know that one of the hardest things to do as men and women is to live our lives completely for You and not for ourselves. We only have one life, one chance to do what we think will make us happy and fulfilled. But help us show You true love and adoration by giving that one life as a sacrifice to You! Because we know that if we don't, we will never find true happiness nor eternal life after all. Indeed, if we try to "save our lives, we will lose them." In Your name, we pray, amen.

Lesson 10: God Has Manufacturer's and Redeemer's Rights

*"I appeal to you therefore, brethren, and beg of you in view of
[all] the mercies of God, to make a decisive dedication of your
bodies [presenting all your members and faculties] as a living
sacrifice, holy (devoted, consecrated) and well pleasing to God,
which is your reasonable (rational, intelligent) service and
spiritual worship."*

Romans 12:1 (AMP)

Notice something else from the Apostle Paul's instructions above
in Romans 12:1: He says that such a complete consecration is our
"reasonable (rational, intelligent) service and spiritual worship."
It is only reasonable that we give ourselves completely to God.
Why? First of all, we should give ourselves to Him because He
has created us. "It is he that hath made us, and not we ourselves;
we are his people..." (Psalm 100:3, KJV). He has Creator's or
manufacturers' rights to us, so it is only reasonable that we give
Him the privilege to exercise those rights.

*The profound, world-changing truth is that we exist only to fulfill
the purpose of God, our Creator. That is our only reason for being
here! Most of us don't really like to hear that. But there is nothing in
this world more important—or more satisfying and fulfilling—than
loving God and dedicating our lives to Him and His cause—no job,
no financial opportunity, no educational attainment, no romantic
endeavor, no social achievement, no artistic endeavor, no achieving
one's dreams, and no other earthly accomplishments.*

But even more than Creator's rights, God has sole right to our lives because He has redeemed our sin-forfeited lives from destruction. As sinners, we were all doomed to death and hell, but by the blood of His Son, Jesus Christ, God bought us back and gave us new lives. So, first of all, that new life belongs to Him. "Or do you not know that your body is the temple of the Holy Spirit Who is in you, Whom you have from God, and you are not your own? For you were bought at a price; therefore glorify God in your body and in your spirit, which are God's" (1 Corinthians 6:19–20, NKJV).

Then, because He first loved us enough to redeem us, our grateful response should be to love Him so much that we *want* to give Him our lives completely. Thus, completely dedicating ourselves to God is only reasonable and intelligent. Holding back on God is unfair to Him and risky business to us: If we knew so well what to do with our lives, we would never have needed Him to save and redeem us from the destruction we had so ignominiously earned and deserved. As Christian rapper Lecrae sang, "If we fought for our rights, we'd be in hell tonight!"

When this type of deep personal consecration is made and maintained, God's Spirit takes possession of that life. He immediately begins the process to produce deliverance, spiritual freedom, inner cleansing, victory over sin and self, emotional healing, and other blessings that enable that person to be "a partaker of the *divine* nature" versus their normal human nature (2 Peter 1:4, KJV). This is how God produces practical holiness in a Christian's daily life. In fact, without a consecration this deep, holy living and discipleship are limited and, ultimately, impossible.

QUESTIONS:

1. Why do you think that it is so difficult for us to admit that we are here *only* to fulfill the purpose and glory of God?
2. Explain why a radically deep consecration is necessary for God to produce holiness in a Christian's life.

PRAYER:

Father, we admit that we are here *only* to fulfill the purpose of God. But help us realize that, because You love us so completely, this purpose is the most pleasant and satisfying life in the world! So, In Jesus' name, help us to be willing to "fit ourselves into Your plans." Amen.

Lesson 11: Step Two: Reaffirm Your Consecration Daily

"And he said to them all, If any man will come after me, let him deny himself, and take up his cross daily, and follow me."

Luke 9:23 (KJV)

"[I assure you] by the pride which I have in you in [your fellowship and union with] Christ Jesus our Lord, that I die daily [I face death every day and die to self]."

1 Corinthians 15:31 (AMP)

Once you have made the radical consecration described in Step One, you can begin to learn an even deeper submission. Complete consecration, as described in Step One, is one thing—one very difficult thing, in fact. But learning submission is another thing, an ongoing process in which your consecration must be reaffirmed *every day* and in every situation.

Following is a practical method to use to reaffirm your consecration: Take a piece of paper and write down everything in your life that is now causing you pain, unhappiness, fear, dissatisfaction, trouble, anxiety, anger, depression, or despair. Be sure to include all the people you can't love and the circumstances you can't tolerate. Include everything from the past that is still bothering you today. Make a complete and descriptive list and label it "Complaint List."

Now for each item on the list, ask yourself the following question: Is this complaint something I brought on myself because of selfish decisions or actions I made outside of the will of God? Only two answers are possible:

1. If the answer is "Yes, I brought this upon myself; it is my fault completely or at least partially," then immediately repent and ask God's forgiveness for that bad move, and He will immediately forgive you. From this time forward, the responsibility for the whole situation is now His: He can either get you out of it at His time or give you divine grace to endure its negative consequences. In either case, He will turn the experience into something that will make you spiritually stronger rather than weaker. Trust Him, and you will be able to relax about it. Your goal is to find peace and happiness in the situation so that it is no longer one of your complaints.

2. The second possible answer is, "No, I did not bring this upon myself. This is not my doing in any way." In that case, it is God's doing. He allowed this trouble or this person into your life, evidently to teach you something, to draw you to Him, or to get you to trust Him more completely. So *"count it all joy"* and *"let patience have her perfect work"* (James 1:4, KJV) in your life.

   Now realize that because of your complete consecration, you are now in the hands of God (not fate, bad luck, or the devil), so absolutely nothing can come your way unless He permits it. As Jesus said to Pilate, "You could have no power at all over Me if it was not given to you by God…" (John 19:11, BBE). Realize that when God gets you into something, He will safely get you out. It is His deal all the way. You were doing His will when whatever happened, happened.

Keep doing His will, and everything will work together for your good. "And we know that all that happens to us is working for our good if we love God and are fitting ourselves into His plans" (Romans 8:28, TLB). Once again, the goal is to find peace and take this complaint off your list.

Go through the entire list of your life's complaints in this manner. If you don't like something, whatever it is, *submit it to God.* When you come to a person you can't love, like, or even *stand*—indeed, some Christians will find people they actually *hate*—submit, not to the person, but to God, by releasing and forgiving that person. Refuse to keep demanding in your mind that they apologize, or respect you, or treat you better. They might not even be around any longer. But your peace and happiness don't depend on them anyway; it's all up to you. Unless you did something to them to make them act that way—for which you must first apologize to them if possible—it is then safe to assume that God permitted them to be difficult in order to make you strong and invulnerable.

QUESTIONS:

1. How long is your Complaint List? What do you plan to do about it?
2. Do you think that it is important for you to try to eliminate your Complaint List? Why or why not?
3. Have you started to relax and feel relieved about this process of giving these things over to God?

PRAYER:

Heavenly Father, we ask Your divine help to eliminate our Complaint Lists. We admit that we cannot find true freedom, happiness, and release from negatives unless we do. So, bless us to give it over to You by using the methods taught in this lesson or any other methods Your divine wisdom teaches us. Turn us into permanent victors, not victims. In Jesus' name, amen.

Lesson 12: Biblical Examples of Radical Submission

"Instead, he emptied himself by taking on the form of a servant, by becoming like other humans, by having a human appearance. He humbled himself by becoming obedient to the point of death, death on a cross."

Philippians 2:7–8 (God's Word)

Joseph, betrayed and sold into slavery by his own brothers, said, "So it was not really you who sent me here, but God" (Genesis 45:8, GNB). King David, while being cursed by Shimei, a soldier loyal to his traitorous son, Absalom, restrained his own soldiers from killing Shimei with the words, "So let him curse, because the Lord hath said unto him, 'Curse David'" (2 Samuel 16:10, KJV). Job, after losing everything he had, sat down, *worshipped,* and, in submission to God, proclaimed, "Naked I came from my mother's womb, and naked shall I return there. The LORD gave, and the LORD has taken away! Blessed be the name of the LORD!" (Job 1:20–21, NKJV).

The Apostle Paul, with his life full of opposite extremes, eventually learned "how to live in poverty or prosperity. No matter what the situation, I've learned the secret of how to live when I'm full or when I'm hungry, when I have too much or when I have too little" (Philippians 4:12, GW).

Jesus Christ Himself, while in His humanity (not His divinity) in the Garden of Gethsemane, feeling awful like all men do when they are facing death, had to pray *three* times before He was truly and absolutely willing to give up His human life! He first asked, in each prayer, if it were possible to avoid death and still remain in the will of the Father, thus indicating that He did not really want to die. *Finally, He became willing to accept death, even an excruciatingly painful death, since God the Father still needed Him to sacrifice Himself.*

He had other options—He could have called "*twelve* legions of angels"—but He had to reject resorting to the divine power at His disposal. He could not make any moves to save Himself or to avoid even a little of the pain or humiliation. Remember how He refused the pain-numbing vinegar and gall while on the cross (Matthew 27:34)? His tormenters mocked, "He saved others, but He cannot save Himself!" (Matthew 27:42, GNB). And how true that was: If He saved Himself, He'd lose all of us! And once He gave up His desire and demands to keep His life, He was able to go through the whole test, no matter how increasingly bad it got. Even while hanging on the cross, He forgave and prayed for His murderers, "Father, forgive them, for they know not what they do" (Luke 23:34, KJV).

So, the secret to being radically submissive to God is found in four critical concepts, three of which are in this verse: "He emptied Himself… He abased and humbled Himself still further, and carried His obedience to God to the extreme point of death" (Philippians 2:8 GW, AMP). These are three different Greek words, but the first step begins with His *emptying*. Once He had *emptied* Himself of His desires to keep His divinity, to avoid pain and humiliation, to not be embarrassed, to maintain His self-respect, to demand His proper recognition as a Divine Being or even as just a regular man, etc., He was able to *humble* Himself still further and *obey*

God, even when it meant He had to die shamefully and naked on a cross. And emptying out one's desires usually feels like dying a death, even if physical death is not involved!

But there is one more—a *fourth*—critical concept of submission, and it explains *why* He did this: Trusting God. He had "*faith* in the operation [wonder-working power] of God to raise Him from the dead" (Colossians 2:12, KJV). He *trusted* that His Father would reward Him as promised, so "He endured (Greek *hupomeno*, 'stayed under') the cross" to achieve the "joy that was set before Him" (Hebrews 12:2, KJV). He found His satisfaction and peace in the fact that He was pleasing God the Father, Who loved Him far too much to allow Him to be really hurt or destroyed. This is an important element in this process because it gives us the *reason* to submit to God. It is built on a loving relationship between you and God and trusts Him to do *only* what is best, absolutely necessary, and really, the quickest and most efficient way to get you to glory and heaven. *Can you trust that?*

That is what it means to radically submit to God.

Real-life Scenarios of Submission

Let's give some real-life examples to make this critical, 4-step submission process even more real. In each of these scenarios, the person is required to first empty, then humble themselves, then obey and learn to trust God:

- A young man feels trapped working for a gospel organization that has become a very unpleasant environment. People are leaving right and left, but he believes God wants him to stay and serve. Sure, he has skills, and he can readily find another job, but God has communicated to him to reject those options, at least for the time being. Should the young man grow resentful and unhappy, constantly pining for another way to serve God, continually wondering if he's wasting his life, worrying about when he will be free to go do his life his way like all his friends seem to be doing? Or should he submit to God in the situation and learn to find happiness there in the will of God?

He should submit: Give up his right to just go do what he wants to do, relinquish his right to avoid looking like an idiot or a glutton for punishment and unpleasantness, and decide that he is going to please God just where God has placed him, even if it means he will humiliatingly stay there for the rest of his life. He should trust that God will only do what is best for him and will never abandon or forget about him. He should determine in his heart that he is going to give God his best as long as he's still at that organization, even if it is an unpleasant environment and might even get worse. He should be able to confidently defend his position, even when his friends think he's stupid for not making the moves they've made. *And he should pray for this complete submission until he truly is at peace about it.*

- A young woman was raped by a close relative and abused during her young years and has grown pretty bitter about it all. She especially hates her mother, who seemed to never care about her and what she was going through. She is now and forever an emotional wreck. But recently, she became a Christian and soon discovers that her anger and bitterness are poisoning every relationship she's ever had. She knows she needs healing but cannot forgive her mother—nor God, for letting it all happen in the first place. In fact, she is driven to control everything and everybody around her because if she doesn't, she is morbidly afraid that she might become a victim of somebody else's selfishness, and she swore that would never happen again. So, she just cannot let go. To let go would make her feel like she was almost dying, that she would be letting certain people go free and that she would lose control over her life.

Should she keep her pride by holding on to her unforgiveness and bitterness, or should she empty herself by giving it all up and letting God, her mother, and everybody else, including herself, go free? If she gives in, she will have to trust God and His love for her, an extremely scary proposition since she has often doubted that love. But being a loving God by definition (whether we always believe it or not!), He will never give us more than we can bear (1 Corinthians 10:13) or take us down an unnecessary detour on our journey to glory. We can trust that He *always* leads us down the safest, most direct path (Psalm 23), even though it might seem otherwise.

- Another young woman wants to get married and have kids, but she knows that God has the right to say who she marries, and she can't just go out and start a relationship with whoever she meets. Besides, all her previous attempts have failed. So, she prays and waits, but God seems to be taking an abysmally long time. Most of her friends have been married for years, and some have had multiple suitors. So, should she get bitter and resentful, feeling rejected, dejected, jealous, and perpetually unhappy? Should she go crazy and just marry the first guy that comes along next, whether or not he's the right man, because "*any* man is better than *no* man at all?" Should she just start acting out sexually in the singles scene? What about her fears that she might be single forever? And *never* have any children? Can she risk waiting for God?

Or should she consecrate to marry nobody if that's how God allows it, and let God be her companion until He sends her somebody, even if it never happens? Should she empty herself by being willing to put her natural desires on hold and concentrate on doing her best for God, with a pleasant, victorious attitude while she waits, quietly trusting that God still has her best interests in mind and has not forgotten her? Can she trust Him that completely so that she is truly *satisfied and happy* to be unmarried until He changes it? This is radical submission. It is no joke.

So, submit to God. Trust Him. Then you will be able to forgive that person, overcome those adverse circumstances, find peace, and remove that situation completely from your Complaint List. *Forgiveness and letting go is a very healing form of submission to God. Unforgiveness and holding on is rebellion, preventing peace of heart and mind.*

The Proof that You Have Submitted

Eventually, if you are truly submitting to God in every area of your life, you will find peace about every complaint you have on your Complaint List. When that is done, you no longer have any complaints! Sure, you have troubles—who doesn't—but none of them are *troubling* you. Indeed, what do you call a "trouble" that no longer troubles you? And what is the result? You are left with a heart completely full of thanksgiving, happiness, and worship.

A heart full of nothing but thanksgiving and worship is the surest indication of a heart fully submitted to God. You have nothing to worry about, nothing to disturb your peace, nothing to be depressed about. You can sing and worship God without a care in the world!

This is what David meant in his most famous psalm, the Twenty-Third Psalm, "The Lord is my Shepherd": "The Lord is my shepherd; I shall not want [i.e., I lack nothing] ... Thou preparedst a table for me in the presence of mine enemies; Thou anointedst my head with oil; my cup runneth over..." (Psalm 23:5, KJV). Like David, in the midst of a life full of natural troubles and unnatural satanic attacks, you are going through on top of the world—free, full of peace, happy, victorious, and unscathed. Unbelievable!

Last, encourage yourself by realizing that "I can be happy because *God* is alive. I can be happy because He loves *me*; *I* am the object of His goodwill and favor. He is taking me to heaven in the absolute best way He can. I can be happy because I am saved, and everything in my life is under God's control and protection. Ultimately nothing and nobody can hurt me..."

This powerful attitude of submission should be used for *everything* that enters your life—the loss of a loved one, a bad relationship, the loss of a job, trouble in the church, a delay in your plans, everyday problems, persecution because you are a Christian who uncompromisingly stands for biblical truth, even adverse driving conditions when you are in a hurry and any other negatives of life. If you do not completely submit to God in it but keep a rebellious or selfish attitude instead and a constant desire to get out of it all, you will find yourself grieving, complaining, resentful, angry, upset, impatient, hateful, bitter, wounded, unable to function, beat down, and affected forever by past and present circumstances. *Do you like those negatives better than perfect peace?!*

Ultimately, you must forgive, forget, accept, resolve, resign, submit, and commit to God everything that happens to you, then move on with life in the name of Jesus. This is the *only* way to keep what happens to you from paralyzing or poisoning your life forever.

Worshipper by Canton Jones
http://www.youtube.com/watch?v=qkUxO6MP3t8

They see me smiling when I hit the street And laugh with everyone
I meet
They see me calm when trouble comes my way Cause I know that it
will be ok
And every single day I wake up, I lift up my hands and I praise you
Cause I know that you will give me life to live
And then, grace and mercy follows so I can do the will
And I'm happy, but to some that's a mystery yeah

[Chorus:] They don't know that I'm a worshipper
And they don't know that I'm in love with you
They don't know that I'm a worshipper
And they don't know that I'm in love with you..

QUESTIONS:

1. Have I ever been cursed or misused in some other way and was able to leave it in the hands of God rather than get back somehow at that person?
2. What four critical concepts are involved in radical submission to God?
3. Paul instructed, "In everything give thanks, for this is the will of God in Christ Jesus concerning you" (1 Thessalonians 5:18, KJV). Have you arrived at the place spiritually where you can truly thank God in everything?

PRAYER:

Father, we can see that submitting to You can require some very difficult decisions. But help us to submit anyway, emptying, humbling ourselves, obeying You no matter how difficult it might be, and enduring the cross by trusting in Your power to bring us through. For Christ's sake, amen.

CHAPTER THREE
THE POWERFUL RESULTS OF RADICAL SUBMISSION

Lesson 13: Falling on the Stone

"And whosoever shall fall on this stone shall be broken: but on whomsoever it shall fall, it will grind him to powder."

Matthew 21:44 (KJV)

There is an important truth to note here: Everything that happens in your life will either *help* you or *hurt* you, depending on how *you* respond to it. Submitting to God protects you from hurt; rebelling leaves you vulnerable. Although He was not completely using this parable in this manner, Jesus mentioned this principle in Matthew 21:44 (AMP): "And whoever falls on this stone will be broken to pieces: but he on whom it falls will be crushed to powder...scattering him as dust." The KJV says that the stone would "grind him to powder."

The kernel of truth is this: When God allows a stumbling stone of any type to be thrown in your way—a loss, a divorce, a loved one's death, some kind of persecution, rejection, or whatever—if you submit to God and voluntarily "fall" on the stone by accepting the adversity as permitted by God, it will indeed "break" your life into pieces. But if you refuse to "fall on the stone" and instead allow the "stone to fall on you"—that is, if you try fighting against the adversity or the people involved and blaming God for allowing it—then the weight and negative effects of the adversity will "grind" your life to "powder." Is it not better to be broken into pieces than to be crushed into powder and scattered as dust?

And it's *your* choice. If you roll with the punches, they will "break" you by bending you, forcing changes and adjustments—usually undesirable—in your life, but ultimately only making you stronger. But if you stand proud and brittle against them, refusing to submit to God in the troubles He allows in your life, refusing to forgive, or refusing to adjust your demands, then those troubles will not merely break you, they will "grind you to powder." They will leave you hurt, damaged, bitter, emotionally and even physically and mentally impaired, and unable to ever rebound or recover—"*scattering you as dust.*" *In every negative situation, you must submit to God for your* own *good and your* own *protection against permanent damage.*

We once counseled a young man who seemed to have only trouble in his life. He couldn't keep a job: Somehow, he would always start believing that the boss and his coworkers were against him, which invariably led to some kind of major confrontation during which he would be fired. He couldn't maintain any healthy relationships. He had close kin, but he blamed them for all of his problems. He lived with permanent anger and resentment. His life was a mess.

When we met him over the phone, he was threatening to jump out of the window of his 25th story apartment. After that crisis was resolved, we got to hear his very sad story: He never knew his father, and his poor single mother allowed the various men she cohabited with (basically for rent and bill money) to physically and sexually abuse her son, the young man. So, he grew up hating her, as well as himself. He tried various methods to find some self-worth. He tried sports and bodybuilding. He tried political and social causes. He changed his name to improve his self-identity. He went to therapists, psychologists, psychiatrists, and other "shrinks," but nothing could shrink his humongous inner turmoil and woundedness. Absolutely no therapies worked. He was still an emotional wreck, ready to jump out his window.

Our belief was that his desperately needed healing could begin if he could somehow find a way to forgive his mother and her boyfriends. We asked if at least he would be *willing* to *try* to forgive them. He let us know very loudly that even the secular psychologists had focused on that point, but absolutely "*No way will I ever forgive her!*" We explained that as long as he held on to *her*, he was actually keeping *himself* from moving past that point. He said he didn't care. We would have to try some other way and some other method.

But there was no other way. There *is* no other method to deal with such bitterness. He needed to recognize that, true, God had allowed this broken world to really hurt him badly and "break his life into pieces," but if he could only be willing to let the other people go, God would keep it from "crushing him to powder and scattering him as dust." God would heal his life. But he continued to refuse. The last time we saw him, he was struggling desperately to keep his sanity. We can only hope that he was able to win that battle, but his chances were not very great.

Listen to William Ebel talk to his own soul in the midst of raging trials and troubles:

Be Still

(by William Ebel, 1911, public domain)
http://library.timelesstruths.org/music/Be_Still/

Oh, be still, thou soul of mine, Thou art not forsaken;
Though the pow'rs of sin may rage, Thou shalt be unshaken.
He who gave His life for thee, Thus permits that thou should be—
For thy good, as thou shalt see—Tempted for a season.

Be courageous, firm, and true, When life's battle's waging;
Oh, be still, my soul, and rest, When the tempest's raging.
He who doth our sorrows share, In His love and tender care
Trials more than thou can bear Will not let thee suffer.

Why should thou so fearful be, At the tempter's roaring?
Simply trust in God alone, Satan's wrath ignoring.
See God's tenderness, and prove With the sainted hosts above,
His unfailing, wondrous love, Ever for thee caring.

Yes, dear Lord, I will be still, I will trust Thee ever;
I'll submit to all Thy will, Cling to Thee forever.
Lord, Thou knowest what is best, Confident in this I'll rest,
Till I dwell with all the blest, And with Thee in heaven.

QUESTIONS:

1. What would you have said to the young man in the story above? What would you have done to help him to forgive?
2. Have you, yourself, or anyone you know been in the situation of being bitter and unable to forgive? How did you get through it? Or *did* you?
3. Identify an area of your life where being ground to powder occurred because you failed to yield the situation to God's control.

PRAYER:

Lord, we can see that forgiving others, letting go, and submitting to You is the path to the freedom and healing we so desperately need and long for. Help us to "fall on the stone" and not allow the "stone to fall on us." One of the two will definitely happen, and we choose the lesser of the evils, though both can be very painful. That's just how life is, and though we might fight hard against it, the way of life is not going to change. It's painful if we do and painful if we don't. O God, we submit to You because we simply cannot fight against You and win. You are God, and You are sovereign. But You also love us too much to forsake us or give us a trial too hard. We trust that today and lay down our arms in surrender. Bless us now In Jesus' name, amen.

Lesson 14: Living Life on the Other Side of Death

"...for we know that the Messiah, who was raised from the dead,
will never die again; death no longer has mastery over him."

Romans 6:9 (ISV)

The awesome power of radical submission lies in this fact: *You can only kill a person once,* and if, by some miraculous power, he comes back to life after you have "killed" him, there is absolutely nothing more you can do to him. This truth is found in Romans 6:9 (NLT): "We are sure of this because Christ rose from the dead, and He will never die again. Death no longer has any power [or 'dominion' (KJV)] over Him."

This is why Jesus Christ came back from the grave proclaiming, "All power in heaven and in earth is given unto Me" (Matthew 28:18, KJV). Satan had done the worst he could possibly do to Jesus, mercilessly torturing and ultimately killing Him. Despite it all, Jesus arose and came back to life! *Now,* what can Satan do to Him? Can he threaten Him with death again? Can he strike fear into Him with pain, or danger, or loss? Jesus could say, "Been there, done that. You made Me sweat before, Satan, but it's no sweat this time, fella! What else do you have in your arsenal?" And the fact is, Satan was completely out of ammunition!

By radically submitting Himself to God and completely dying to this world, Jesus was ushered into the most powerful position a human being can ever be in: *Living life on the other side of death*!

The truth is a person who has truly died to himself and crucified his flesh can live beyond the corrupting reach of the fear of death. In other words, a "dead" man does not respond to the fear of death—the threat of loss, trouble, danger, social or economic pressure, or even physical death itself—because he is already dead! Satan has no power over him to pull or push him around with the fear of death. *This is the most powerful position in the world to be in. And that is because the Resurrected Life is the most powerful life in the world. And nobody can experience a resurrection until they have first died!*

Paul states this very well in Hebrews 2:14–15 (NIV): "Since the children have flesh and blood, He too shared in their humanity so that by His death He might destroy him who holds the power of death—that is, the devil—and free those who all their lives were held in slavery by their fear of death."

The Amplified Bible says "that by [going through] death," Jesus would "bring to naught and make of no effect him who had the power of death." He went "through" death as if it were a tunnel, and came out on the other side, forever untouchable and even unlimited by the laws of nature. We are to die to ourselves and be "buried with Him," then raised by His resurrection to "walk in newness of life," which is symbolized by water baptism (Romans 6:1–6).

And this "newness of life" is the term used to describe radical Christianity and true discipleship: Living life on the other side of death. What's so new about a life that is still being lived with the scars of the past, the anxiety of the present, and the fear of the future? *Only after you die to this life through submission to God are you free to really live.*

Obviously, Satan's power over mankind is centered in his ability to scare us into compliance with his wishes by threatening us with death, loss, suffering, rejection, insecurity, danger, pain, purposelessness, fear of missing some wonderful, life-enhancing opportunity, and other common negatives which we so greatly want to avoid. We typically spend our lives struggling to avoid death in its various forms, making all kinds of sinful, selfish compromises to save and enhance our lives. Unfortunately, this violates one of Jesus' greatest principles: "Those who want to save their lives will lose them. But those who lose their lives for Me will save them" (Luke 9:24, GW; 17:33, GW; Matthew 16:25, GW; Mark 8:35, GW).

But by dying to ourselves through absolute submission to God, Jesus Christ lifts us *beyond* that fear of death so that we can live powerful lives of holiness and obedience to God alone. *A person who has lost it all has nothing more to lose!*

Fear, the dominant human motivator, completely dissipates when you realize *that* "your life is hid with Christ in God" (Colossians 3:3, KJV); that is, everything in your life has been yielded and submitted into God's will. You have no life that you have deliberately left outside of the will, Word, and Way of God.

"What have I to dread, what have I to fear, leaning on the everlasting arms?" the old hymn, "*What A Fellowship*," asks. You are *hiding* in the arms of God, protected from everything that can really hurt you. This is a place—the only place on earth—of true relaxation. Whatever God wants—whatever He wants to do with you, *with* your life, *in* your life, *to* your life—is just fine with you. Whether you live or die, whether you prosper or suffer, whether you experience abundance or deprivation, whether you gain or lose, whether you find fame and acceptance or toil forever as an unknown—all is still in the hands of God.

Thus, fear is cast out—"Perfect love casts out fear" (1 John 4:18, KJV)—and your peace and happiness are permanent and invulnerable.

A Little Part of His Plan

"I find no need to worry when things get out of hand.
Why should I lose my courage? It's all still in His plan.
Just give me faith to trust You, to trust when I can't trace,
For I know everything to be A little part of Your plan for me."[1]

A missionary group was on its way to a wild, dangerous region from which few men had ever returned. One of their friends, fearing for their safety, tried to persuade them not to go with the words, "Don't you know you might die there?" The missionaries replied, "We died before we ever left home." *A person who no longer has fear is the most powerful person on earth and also the most dangerous for Jesus Christ and His eternal Kingdom! Like a "gospel terrorist," that person will do absolutely anything for God! He will be a "holy terror" to the kingdom of Satan & hell! (And, of course, we are talking only about righteousness here.)*

In like manner, we might say that Jesus "died" in the Garden of Gethsemane long before He was actually nailed to the cross. Once a person undergoes this "death," Satan ceases to have any power over him or her. You can only kill a person once. This is the awesome, life-changing power of radical submission to God!

QUESTIONS:

1. Is it too strong to teach and believe that a radical Christian should "die" to himself in order to truly please God? Can you please God at all times if you have not died to yourself?
2. What will eventually happen if a person tries to go through life still "alive?"
3. Identify an area of your life where you have found "true relaxation" from any fear whatsoever because you are "leaning on the Everlasting Arms…"

PRAYER:

Lord, help us to die to our own desires, wishes, whims, demands, plans, dreams, and ambitions, so we can start living life on the other side of death. Let us die with Christ to sin and to our own selves and begin to live Your Resurrected Life on a daily basis. In Jesus' name, amen.

Lesson 15: "He Hath Nothing in Me"

"Everyone is tempted by his own desires as they lure him away and trap him."

James 1:14 (GW)

Right before He went to the cross, Jesus gave us the one secret to permanent and impenetrable victory over the devil. "Hereafter I will not talk much with you," He told His disciples, "for the prince of this world cometh, and hath nothing in Me" (John 14:30, KJV). The Amplified version says it this way: "I will not talk with you much more, for the prince (evil genius, ruler) of the world is coming. And he has no claim on Me—he has nothing in common with Me, there is nothing in Me that belongs to him, he has no power over Me."

This point is the greatest secret to Christian victory ever given: The only way we can have victory over the devil is if he can find nothing in *us* that belongs to *him*. Satan, as the "prince of this world," has been given authority over everything belonging to this world. Selfishness is the basic ingredient of this world, according to 1 John 2:15–17: All that is in the world is "the lust of the flesh [craving for sensual gratification], and the lust of the eyes [greedy longings of the mind] and the pride of life [assurance in one's own resources or in the stability of earthly things] …" (AMP). So, if we allow selfishness in any form to lie around in our hearts,

Satan has authority over it and will use that selfishness to control and defeat us.

For example, if Jesus Himself had allowed the natural human desire for respect to remain in His heart, Satan would have been able to manipulate that desire to prevent Jesus from going to the cross. Jesus definitely would have come down from the cross when His enemies taunted Him to do so, just to satisfy His human desire for respect and vengeance.

But the truth was that Jesus had "emptied Himself," not only of His right to be equal with God but also of His natural human desire to stay alive and to receive respect and decent treatment from other people. This secret is stated plainly in Philippians 2:7: "But [He] emptied Himself…" (ASV). "But [He] stripped Himself [of all privileges and rightful dignity]…" (AMP). So, Satan didn't "own" anything within Jesus to use against Him.

The problem with Christians today is that very few of us are truly emptied of ourselves. Instead, we are literally *full* of ourselves. Too many of us, leaders and laypeople alike, are filled to the brim with our natural human ambitions, our own desires, our demand for respect, our wants, our whims, our wishes, our goals for personal fulfillment, our need for comfort, convenience, safety, and security, and such like.

Thus, Satan is easily able to manipulate our inner selfishness to tempt us, to defeat us, and to drag our Christian witness through the mud. These are the strings that keep us attached like puppets to the earthly things that Satan, the master puppeteer, uses to get us to do his will. We make the devil's job far too easy. But to be Christ-like and victorious, we must detach ourselves and empty ourselves and be able to say like Jesus, "The devil shall find nothing that belongs to *him* in *me*." Radical submission empties you of yourself.

For more on this subject, consider James 1:21 (AMP): "But every person is tempted when he is drawn away, enticed and baited by his own evil desire (lust, passions)." In other words, our own inward desires are what enable us to be drawn away and tempted to act evil or selfish. The devil can tempt you *only* through the desires you have within your own self. It's something *in you* that goes after his bait. You can't catch a fish if he's not hungry! You can't bribe an official if he's satisfied with the salary he's already making. You can't get a man to chase after another man's wife if he's satisfied with his own wife.

Though temptation itself is not a sin, it shows you where you have an internal weakness that you must be especially careful of. So then, you are able to identify where you have a problem and what you need to work on, i.e., either get rid of or place under the Spirit's control. Thus, because he's always probing to expose our weaknesses, we might say that Satan actually does us a favor when he tempts us, falling right into the plans of God! He's quite a good devil!

QUESTIONS:

1. What is the greatest secret to Christian victory that has ever been given?
2. Have you located and become aware of desires within yourself that can potentially lead you away into evil? What do you plan to do about these desires?

PRAYER:

Lord Jesus, make us more aware of the many areas in which we are spiritually weak. If these weaknesses are in areas that are natural and cannot be removed, help us to place these things under the control of Your Holy Spirit. But if these areas involve something we have acquired a taste and desire for, then help us to give up these desires and allow You to remove them. For Christ's sake, amen.

Lesson 16: What Is Real Humility?

"And being found in fashion as a man, He humbled Himself, and became obedient unto death, even the death of the cross."

Philippians 2:8 (KJV)

The manifestation or proof of being emptied of oneself is the true definition of humility. Once Jesus "emptied Himself," He was able to "humble Himself." Only then was He able to "obey," even when it meant dying on the cross.

To empty yourself means to relinquish your grasp on your rights and desires, i.e., to give them up. Notice the wording of Philippians 2:6–7 in the Amplified: "Who, although being essentially one with God and in the form of God [possessing the fullness of the attributes which make God God], did not think this equality with God was a thing to be eagerly grasped or retained, But stripped Himself [of all privileges and rightful dignity], so as to assume the guise of a servant (slave), in that He became like men and was born a human being. And after He had appeared in human form, He abased and humbled Himself [still further] and carried His obedience to the extreme of death, even the death of the cross!" And the Greek word translated "stripped" in the Amplified and "made Himself of no reputation" in the King James Version is *kenoo*, meaning to "make empty or void." So, Jesus did not grasp and hold to His rights and dignity of being Divinity but emptied Himself.

Then, once His Divine rights and desires were emptied out, He was able to "humble" Himself. That is, *He* "*lowered and abased or depressed*" *Himself in relation to all others*, the meaning of the Greek word *tapeinoo*. First of all, He allowed Himself to become another form, "the guise of a slave," a human being, then "He abased and humbled Himself still further" by becoming obedient to die on the cross. *So being able to humble yourself is proof and manifestation that you have emptied yourself.*

Keep in mind the unseen, *assumed* truth that explains *why* Jesus was willing to empty, humble, and obey: He had absolute faith in His Father's love (John 5:20) and His Father's power (Colossians 2:12). This is the basis for such radical submission. Therefore, He was willing to give it all up and lay it all down because He was convinced that His Father would reward Him and never let Him perish (Hebrews 12:1–4).

Thus, humility is not just *one* of the spiritual graces. *It is the seedbed from which all other spiritual graces spring and grow.* After He humbled Himself, Jesus was able to show *all* of the other graces: Love for His persecutors, forgiveness, patience, longsuffering, peace, incredible calmness, faith in God, the ability to hold His tongue (KJV, "held on to His peace"), etc. All of these graces are forms of *obedience* to God: The ability to shut up when the Holy Spirit tells us we need to be quiet, the grace to be self-controlled, patient, and calm when craziness is happening all around, the God-like power to show love and forgiveness to those who are persecuting, abusing, or taking unfair advantage of us, etc.

Thus, this is the practical truth: Whenever we cannot obey God by exhibiting these graces, the problem is always that we haven't humbled or lowered ourselves far enough because we haven't emptied ourselves of our rights and desires completely enough. And this goes right back to our lack of "Faith, which is based on love" (Galatians 5:6).

The lyrics of a song written by William G. Schell, "Humility," in an old Church of God hymnal, "Evening Light Songs," describe these profound truths:

Humility, thou secret vale, unknown to proud in heart,
Where showers of blessing never fail, and glories never depart.
Humility, how pure thy place! *Thou seat of holiness!*
Thou door of entrance into grace and everlasting bliss!

Humility, how calm the breast that knows thy peace sublime!
Within thy courts our perfect rest grows sweeter all the time.

Humility, thou shoreless sea of perfect love so deep!
Thy crystal waters cover me, my helpless soul to keep.

Oh, make thy blest abode with me, thou angel of the sky.
If I may ever dwell with thee, my soul shall never die.

What Is Pride?

If humility is the manifestation and proof of being self-emptied, it should be obvious that pride, generally considered to be the opposite of humility, is merely the *natural state of not being emptied of oneself.* We, as humans, are *naturally* filled with pride. Humility, however, is not natural. It can only be accomplished deliberately and only by God's grace.

All spiritual graces spring from humility, as proven above. *All lack of spiritual graces spring from pride.* Humility gives us unlimited spiritual power and ability; pride keeps us forever vulnerable to the devil and his ability to manipulate human beings.

Like Christ, the humble, self-emptied person can forgive, sincerely "pray for those who spitefully use" him (Matthew 5:44,

KJV) and move on with life under all circumstances. But the proud, non-emptied person *cannot* forgive, *cannot* sincerely pray for his enemies, and is doomed to spend lots of time moping, complaining, rehashing events in his mind, and hoping for retaliation, vindication, or getting even. Pride also manifests itself through conceit, cynicism, biting sarcasm, despising others, being hard-hearted and unforgiving, not having mercy on others, being dishonest with God, and other forms of hidden bitterness. Many Christians live this way every day, contrary to the Spirit of Christ and the love and softness of heart He showed.

The humble person can live holy and lovingly; the proud person is driven to live selfishly. That is because the humble person is truly free, but the proud person is a slave to his own selfish desires and to the evil being who controls such.

What Is the Relationship between Humility and Agape Love?

Thus, we can describe the relationship between humility and *agape* love in the following manner. Think of a coin having two sides, heads and tails. *Agape* love is heads, and humility is tails. All coins must have both. But *agape* is what God alone does—*agape* comes *only* from God—while humility is what man does. *That is, when man empties and humbles himself, God's agape love can then manifest itself—and not until then.* Notice 1 Corinthians 13. When Paul describes *agape* love, he really seems to describe humility from man's perspective: "Love suffers long… Love is not boastful or vainglorious, does not display itself haughtily… Love is not conceited… Love does not insist on its own rights or its own way, for it is not self-seeking…"

Man's humility, i.e., self-emptying and lowering himself, enables God's *agape* love to be expressed. It is automatic: When we are emptied of self, then *agape* love can and will flow into and through us—no need to pray for patience or the ability to forgive. Just humble yourself, and His patience will take over. No need to worry about whether you can find grace to go through a hard trial or have peace in the midst of a super-long tribulation. Simply empty and humble yourself, and God's divine love will automatically flow through you with power, grace, endurance, peace, and joy. Of course, this is easier said than done, but if you do your part (humility), He will unfailingly do His part (*agape* love).

QUESTIONS:

1. Looking back, can you see instances in the process you have failed to either empty, humble, obey, or trust the Father's love? What do you plan to do about this?

PRAYER:

Oh, Father, thank You for giving us Your Word and helping us to analyze this critical process of emptying, humbling, obeying, and trusting. Now help us to practice these wonderful truths every day in the form of *agape* love. In the name of our Lord Jesus Christ, amen.

Lesson 17: Perfect Submission, All Is at Rest

"He that dwelleth in the secret place of the most High shall abide under the shadow of the Almighty. I will say of the LORD, He is my refuge and my fortress: my God; in him will I trust."

Psalm 91:1–2

Many Christian songwriters throughout history have sung about submission, but listen to the words of *"Blessed Assurance,"* one of the most beloved hymns of the Christian faith, by one of its best songwriters, Fanny Crosby:

> "Perfect submission, perfect delight!
> Visions of rapture now burst on my sight.
> Angels descending bring from above
> Echoes of mercy, visions of love.
>
> Perfect submission; all is at rest,
> I in my Savior am happy and blest.
> Watching and waiting, looking above,
> Filled with His goodness, lost in His love."[2]

The above practice of radical submission is what she was singing about. She went blind at age three, the victim of a quack doctor. Yet, she learned to be happy every day by learning submission to God. Every day she wrote a song or two—over 2,000 total! The more perfect your submission, the more perfect your delight will be. The more perfect your submission, the more everything in your life will be at rest.

We live in a world of restless, stressed-out, constantly moving, dissatisfied, wound-driven, depressed, craving, complaining, anxious, selfishness-manifesting, weak, non-victorious, resentful, revengeful, even fighting Christians, and the whole reason is a pervasive lack of radical submission to God. *Perfect submission is that "secret place of the Most High."*

The natural state of the true disciple is to be at rest in every circumstance of life. The Psalmist, David, once longed like most of us human beings, *"Oh that I had wings like a dove! for then would I fly away and be at rest"* (Psalm 55:6, KJV). But it doesn't require an escape from your circumstances to find rest—only perfect submission. Spiritual equilibrium, happiness, and consistency have always been God's original intention for His children—inward satisfaction, freedom from worry, lack of inner turmoil, confident trust in God, being at peace with God and man. Any condition less than this means that, in some area of your life, you need to submit to God, deny self, resist the devil, and find peace. Don't settle for less than this, your full privilege and birthright in Christ.

George Douglas Watson, a Wesleyan Methodist pastor, was one of the most influential preachers of the late 1800s holiness movement in America. He was known as the "Apostle to the Sanctified." Listen to one of his most popular hymns, no doubt learned from practicing radical submission to the will of God:

The Bondage of Love

O sweet will of God! thou hast girded me round
Like the deep moving currents that girdle the sea.
With omnipotent Love is my poor nature bound,
And this bondage to Love sets me perfectly free!

For years my soul wrestled with vague discontent,
That like a sad angel overshadowed my way.
God's light in my soul with the darkness was blent,
And my heart ever longed for an unclouded day.

And now I have flung myself recklessly out,
Like a chip on the stream of the Infinite Will.
I pass the rough rocks with a smile and a shout,
And I just let my God His dear purpose fulfill!

Forever I choose the good will of my God,
Its holy, deep riches to love and to know.
The serfdom of love to so sweeten the rod,
That its touch maketh rivers of honey to flow.

Roll on, checkered seasons, bring smiles or bring tears,
My soul sweetly sails on an infinite tide!
I shall soon touch the shores of eternity's years,
And near the white throne of my Savior abide!

Hallelujah! Hallelujah! My soul is now free!
For the precious blood of Jesus cleanseth even me.

The peace and rest that come from submitting to the will of God are indeed very profound! How many Christians today have reached the point in their spiritual relationship with God that they can truthfully say with George Watson, *"And now I have flung myself recklessly out"* on the infinite, loving will of God, knowing that such a move is the wisest move a person could possibly make and is not really reckless at all? How many Christians do you know who are able to just *"pass the rough rocks [of life] with a smile and a shout"* by being willing to just let God fulfill His loving purpose in their lives? *That* is radical submission, the source of true happiness.

QUESTIONS:

1. Looking at Mrs. Fanny J Crosby's lyrics, what truths do you see in the phrase, "Perfect submission, perfect delight!"? What do you see in the phrase, "Perfect submission, all is at rest"?
2. Have *you* settled for less than "perfect delight" and "all is at rest"?

PRAYER:

Father God, let us find the "secret place of the Most High"—and "dwell" there, stay there, where we are protected and sheltered from all harm and distress. Help us to use You fully as the refuge You promised to be, "passing the rough rocks with a smile and a shout," and finding peace, strength, and deliverance from fear and restlessness (Psalm 46). In His name, amen.

Lesson 18: When God Hijacks Your Life

"And in the sixth month the angel Gabriel was sent from God unto a city of Galilee, named Nazareth, to a virgin espoused to a man whose name was Joseph, of the house of David; and the virgin's name was Mary. And the angel came in unto her, and said, 'Hail, thou that art highly favored, the Lord is with thee: blessed art thou among women.'

And when she saw him, she was troubled at his saying, and cast in her mind what manner of salutation this should be. And the angel said unto her, 'Fear not, Mary: for thou hast found favor with God. And, behold, thou shalt conceive in thy womb, and bring forth a son, and shalt call his name JESUS. He shall be great, and shall be called the Son of the Highest: and the Lord God shall give unto him the throne of his father David: And he shall reign over the house of Jacob forever; and of his kingdom there shall be no end.'

Then said Mary unto the angel, 'How shall this be, seeing I know not a man?'

And the angel answered and said unto her, 'The Holy Ghost shall come upon thee, and the power of the Highest shall overshadow thee: therefore also that holy thing which shall be born of thee shall be called the Son of God. And, behold, thy Cousin Elisabeth, she hath also conceived a son in her old age: and this is the sixth month with her, who was called barren. For with God nothing shall be impossible.'

And Mary said, 'Behold the handmaid of the Lord; be it unto me according to thy word.' And the angel departed from her."

Luke 1:26–38

During each Christmas season, we get to meditate once again on a very special young woman, Mary, the mother of Jesus the Messiah. Let's imagine what this would mean to us today: Here's this little fifteen, sixteen-year-old girl, nobody special, minding her own business, living as righteously as she can, engaged to be married to a nice working-class gentleman, and expecting to have a normal little life raising her children in a nice little working-class neighborhood in the nothing-special-about-it city of Nazareth. Then, one day from out of nowhere, it seems, an angel appears and makes this incredible annunciation that simply blasts her expectations of normalcy to smithereens.

So, God just hijacks her life! Like the little life sparked within her, increasingly growing bigger and bigger until it literally takes over her body, this monumental burden just takes over her whole existence. She no longer belongs to herself at all. All her own expectations and ambitions have to move over and are completely replaced by *God's* expectations and ambitions. She has no life now—except the life God has chosen for her. Her marriage dreams, her relationships with every other person in her life, her reputation, her present, her future, her purpose for living—her entire physical, spiritual, and emotional life is forever, unalterably, and radically changed, co-opted by God without Him asking her anything!

Likewise, Joseph's life is hijacked too. Whatever he had in mind for his life, that's over, suddenly and rudely replaced by the burden and calling of being stepfather to the Son of God! Man, Joseph, you are gonna be the laughingstock of the town, fella. Surely you aren't gonna let yourself be suckered into believing that stuff about Mary's "Immaculate Conception," are you? Everybody can see that she cheated on you and got pregnant! What you gonna do, man?!

But notice the responses of these two righteous people. Mary, knowing at least a few of the awful ramifications of this new, hijacked life, meekly says, "Behold, I am the handmaiden, the '*doule,*' *the female slave*, of the Lord. Let it happen to me just as you have said." And Joseph, after the angel appears to him in a dream, rises from his sleep and does just what the angel of the Lord told him to do, by marrying Mary, covering her potential shame, refusing to sleep with her until she gives birth, then obediently naming her child "Jesus" as he was instructed (Matthew 1:24–25). And the rest is "His Story!"

It's probably good that God chose for His Son to be born two thousand years ago because He might have a much more difficult task finding people like this in today's Christian world. Not very many people are willing to let God hijack their lives—without even asking their permission. God and His big ideas, and I just happen to be the little guinea pig! What's that all about? How fair is *that?*

How many of us would just quietly and meekly allow God the privilege to hijack our lives and turn them completely into something *He* has in mind? How many of us are willing and content to live *only* the life that God alone has chosen and charted for us? *How many of us must be dragged, kicking and screaming, into the will of God?! Lord, have mercy!*

But this is the awesome truth of the matter: We are *all* pregnant with something special from God, something divinely sparked within us by the Holy Spirit. We *all* have Christ being formed in us (Galatians 4:19; Colossians 1:27). We *all* have a special calling upon our lives (2 Timothy 1:9; Hebrews 3:1; Ephesians 4:4; 2 Peter 1:10), and as called believers, we *all* have something special that we are duty-bound to offer to this world. We *all* have a burden, a gifting, a vision, a divine responsibility, a spiritual assignment, a message from God, a "word of wisdom or knowledge" (1 Corinthians 12:8), a sacred charge that God expects to take over our lives (1 Corinthians 9:17; 12:7; Matthew 25:15; Romans 12:6; Ephesians 4:7; 1 Peter 4:10). We *all*, like Paul, have been "apprehended, seized, and arrested by Christ" for a specific purpose (Philippians 3:12). Like Mary, we *all* should have no life now—except the life God has chosen for us (Galatians 2:20). We *all* are not our own (1 Corinthians 6:19–20). Jesus' blood has bought *all* of us, and God's grace and gifting now *totally* own us *all*. But how many of us are willing to be totally owned by the calling of God?

Are you ready to submit to that reality? Will you draw back (Hebrews 10:38–39) and insist on living your Christian life your own way—or *God's*? Are you still fighting the fact that yours is a hijacked life? *It's time to get used to it because living a hijacked life is* supposed *to be the normal Christian experience!* That *is the life that will bear fruit for the kingdom. That is the life that will truly amaze the world, even the church world!*

QUESTIONS:

1. Do you agree or disagree with this statement: "The reason most Christian lives are unfruitful is because they never give God the chance to hijack and just take over their lives!"?
2. What specific gifts and callings are you "pregnant" with, and what are you doing about it?
3. When was the first time your life was "hijacked" and you realized that God was doing something not normal in your life?

PRAYER:

Oh, Lord, forgive us for holding back and hoarding our own lives for ourselves. Help us to say with Mary, "I am the slave of the Lord!" Direct us and inspire us to get moving on the callings you have placed upon our lives. Keep us from all excuses and procrastinations. And let us start today! For Christ and the Kingdom, amen.

Lesson 19: The Life of the World Springs from the Death of Christ's Body

"I assure you, most solemnly I tell you, Unless a grain of wheat falls into the earth and dies, it remains [just one grain; it never becomes more but lives] by itself alone. But if it dies, it produces many others and yields a rich harvest."

John 12:24 (AMP)

In John 12:24, Jesus states plainly the major principle on which the salvation of the world is based: *The world is given eternal life through the death and spilt blood of the Body of Christ.* And He solemnizes it and guarantees its truthfulness by prefixing to it one of His famous "Verily verily's," that is, *"I assure you, I most solemnly tell you, I can guarantee this truth."* In other words, it is impossible to get around this fact of Truth.

This principle of life emanating from death applies on every level. It applied to Jesus directly: Unless He died, the world could not be saved. He could bring life to others only by dying on the Cross. If He hadn't given up His life, then He would have merely been one great solitary life, never bearing the fruit of giving life to others. "This is My body which is given for you," He told His disciples (Luke 22:19). His murderers mocked while He hung on the cross, "He saved others; Himself He cannot save" (Mark 15:31). And how true were their words: If He had saved Himself, He would not have been able to save others.

This principle also applies to the Body of Christ in the world since that time. *The world can only be saved through the death of the collective Body of Christ.* If we save ourselves, we will never save the world. If we remain preoccupied with our own prosperity and personal development, we will never be able to make the tremendous sacrifices required to get the Gospel of Jesus Christ into the hearts and minds of the lost world. We will never be able to save our neighbors. *This world will be converted only as rapidly as and to the degree in which the Body of Christ—the Church—dies to itself.*

In fact, this is the only reason the world is not saved right now, and evil seems to be exponentially increasing: *The Church, in general, has grown rather self-satisfied and refuses to die.* We want to live. So we do, largely for ourselves. But God is still calling for us to die.

Now because this principle applies to the Body of Christ as a whole, it also applies to the individual members who make up that Body of Christ in this world. "So we constantly experience the death of Jesus in our own bodies," Paul wrote the Corinthian church, "but this is so that the life of Jesus can also be seen in our bodies. We are alive, but for Jesus, we are always in danger of death so that the life of Jesus can be seen in our bodies that die. So death is working in us, but the result is that life is working in you" (2 Corinthians 4:12, ERV).

The journey to salvation for Paul himself began at the murder of Stephen, where Saul, who became Paul, stood holding the coats of those stoning Stephen, watching him die like Jesus died, crying, "Lord Jesus, receive my spirit; lay not this sin to their charge" (Acts 7:59–60, KJV). From Stephen's perfectly-timed, God-ordained death, the Christian faith spread like wildfire out into the Roman world as the disciples ran for their lives from Jerusalem, taking their new faith with them wherever they settled. And thus, the

Christian faith, at first a little offshoot of Judaism limited to the small country of Palestine, became and continues to be, 2,000 years later, an international phenomenon and force for life.

Paul's life—and the lives of all the Apostles and early Christians—are very good examples of individuals giving up themselves so that others could have eternal life. They brought the Gospel down to our generation. These men and women actually rejoiced in their self-denial and suffering for Christ: "And they departed from the presence of the council, rejoicing that they were counted worthy to suffer shame for His Name" (Acts 5:41).

Later, Paul testified that "Yes, all the things I once thought were so important are gone from my life. Compared to the high privilege of knowing Christ Jesus as my Master, firsthand, everything I once thought I had going for me is insignificant—dog dung. I've dumped it all in the trash so that I could embrace Christ and be embraced by Him. I didn't want some petty, inferior brand of righteousness that comes from keeping a list of rules when I could get the robust kind that comes from trusting Christ—God's righteousness. I gave up all that inferior stuff so I could know Christ personally, experience His resurrection power, be a partner in [i.e., fellowship] His suffering, and go all the way with Him to death itself. If there was any way to get in on the resurrection from the dead, I wanted to do it" (Philippians 3:8–11, The Message).

I once saw a tribute to Janusz Korczak, a Polish-Jewish man who led 192 Jewish orphans to the gas chamber in the infamous Treblinka extermination camp in 1942 during the Holocaust. The truth was, he had been given many opportunities to save himself, but he refused to abandon his children. Instead, he walked to the gas chamber with them, holding their hands, soothing their fears, and keeping up their spirits until the end. These were his words:

"I exist not to be loved and admired, but to love and act. It is not the duty of those around me to love me. Rather, it is my duty to be concerned about the world, about man[kind]." How much Janusz Korczak sounded like Jesus Christ: "Do as I did: The Son of Man did not come for people to serve him. He came to serve others and to give his life to save many people" (Matthew 20:28, ERV).

And so today, God calls for His children to deny themselves, to live by a different, other-worldly value system, to bypass many of the prosperous opportunities the world has to offer, to suffer when necessary, to give copious amounts of time, money, and tireless effort, and to make incredible sacrifices—all for the salvation of the world around us. "You didn't choose Me, remember; I chose you, and put you in the world to bear fruit, fruit that won't spoil, [but would last]," Jesus told His disciples (John 15:16, The Message).

Somebody must "Go" (Matthew 28:19–20, KJV)! But if we go for God, we won't be able to keep living for ourselves. Somebody has got to avoid getting trapped by materialism, forego big-time careers, and give up building their secure little nest eggs so that people who need to know Him will truly get the chance to know Him. Somebody has got to radically concentrate on eternal matters—and put earthly matters on the back burner. *Who's* going to do that? Somebody has got to pay the price for dying souls, and the price continues to be, as it was in the beginning, the *life* of the Body of Christ.

Somebody has got to be like Isaiah, who, when asked by the Lord, "Whom can I send, and who will go for us?" answered, "Here am I. Send me!" (Isaiah 6:8). Here we are, after 2,000 years of Christianity, and it is estimated that 3.2 *billion* people, almost 40 percent of the world's population, still have never heard of Jesus Christ! *How can that be possible? Quite shameful!*

The old hymn by Thomas Shepherd says it all succinctly: "Must Jesus bear the cross alone and all the world go free? No, there's a cross for everyone, and there's a cross for me." This includes *you and me*, brothers and sisters, everyone who calls Jesus their Lord!

Listen, you don't have to "go across the sea" or die at the hands of cannibals in some far-off Third-World wilderness! All you need to do is go across the street! Or go to the "other side" of town. All you need to do is start changing your own neighborhood! All you must be willing to do is change your busy, self-focused, preprogrammed life to include more time, money, and physical strength for God and His work. All you need to do is to go out of your way and leave your comfort zone to love somebody who is dying to receive a touch from heaven. Everybody in the Body does not have to be some world-class missionary. But all of us can do the simple stuff.

Why does this sound so strange and unfamiliar and fanatical? So radical? It is because so much of Christianity, especially here in America, has bought into the misleading concept that the main purpose of salvation is for God to pour out lots of blessings on you, to keep bad things from happening to you, and to ensure your perpetual comfort and ease. God has become the great "Big Blessing Machine in the Sky."

This concept must be utterly renounced and rejected. *But that can only be done by those who daily practice radical submission to God, offering themselves as "living sacrifices" to Jesus Christ, no strings attached.* They are the ones who will help fulfill His prayer, "Thy Kingdom come. Thy will be done in earth, as it is in heaven" (Matthew 6:10, KJV).

QUESTIONS:

1. Ask yourself this question: "What am *I* doing, what am *I* giving up, and what am *I* dying to that will help bring salvation to the lost world around me, at home and abroad?"
2. Can you see areas of your life where you appear to have bought into the "Big Blessing Machine" mentality? If so, how will you fix that?

PRAYER:

Heaven Father, I realize now more than ever that You saved me to use me in some way to help save others. Forgive me for letting this life distract me from Your divine, eternal purposes. Reveal to me what You want me to do and how You want me to live so that I truly become an "instrument of Your peace and righteousness." Use me to produce fruit for You. For Your Kingdom's sake and in Jesus' name, amen.

Lesson 20: The Prince of Peace's Gift to the World

"Peace I leave with you, My peace I give unto you…"

John 14:27 (KJV)

Jesus is called the "Prince of Peace," simply for the reason that peace is the gift He came to bring to everyone in the world. Few find that peace, but His disciples certainly should. "I am leaving you with a gift—peace of mind and heart," Jesus said (John 14:27 TLB). "And the peace I give isn't fragile like the peace the world gives. So don't be troubled or afraid."

The "peace" that the world gives depends on achieving perfect and ideal circumstances in one's life, but Jesus' peace depends only on Him and His steady love for us. Most Christians literally kill themselves struggling to control circumstances, to change other people (or run from the difficult ones or even cuss them out!), and to create perfect or good enough conditions so we can finally relax and find some peace and happiness. We die trying to live when Jesus just wants us to have a life of peace and happiness right where we are.

He's Everything That I Need

"Well, there's no one like Jesus to still life's sea,
And bring an unspeakable peace.
Yes, a peace not depending on my troubles relenting,
But all on His sweet love to me."[3]

Or the old gospel favorite, "*Blessed Quietness*," by Mrs. M. P. Ferguson:

"Joys are flowing like a river, Since the Comforter has come. He abides with us forever, Makes the trusting heart His home."

Everything is turned to gladness, All around this glorious Guest. Banished unbelief and sadness, All is perfect peace and rest.

Blessed quietness, holy quietness, Blest assurance in my soul! On the stormy sea, *Jesus speaks to me*, And the billows cease to roll."

Notice that the lyricist said, "Jesus speaks to *me*"—not to the stormy sea—"and the billows cease to roll." The truth is, when the Prince of Peace speaks sweet peace to *me*, it doesn't matter at all what might still be happening out on the stormy sea!

His Name Is Jesus

"And now that I've found Him, *real* peace is mine!
The world may be raging, but *I'm* doing fine!
There's nothing quite like Him, this Savior divine!
His name is Jesus, God's Gift from above.

QUESTIONS:

1. What are the typical "billows" and "storms" in your life from day to day?
2. Define and describe what peace means to you.

PRAYER:

Heavenly Father, we are so glad that You came to peace and happiness to this restless world, but most of all, to our restless hearts. Help us to always "let the peace of God rule in our hearts" (Colossians 3:15). In Jesus' name, amen.

Lesson 21: You Are Not the Man for the Job

*" And God blessed them, and God said unto them, Be fruitful,
and multiply, and replenish the earth, and subdue it: and have
dominion over the fish of the sea, and over the fowl of the air,
and over every living thing that moves upon the earth."*

Genesis 1:28 (KJV)

Another way to describe the problem we human beings have is
by going back to the Garden of Eden and looking at what really
happened there. God had made people for His pleasure (Revelation 4:11, KJV) to manage the world for Him. "God blessed them
and said, 'Be fertile, increase in number, fill the earth, and be its
master. Rule the fish in the sea, the birds in the sky, and all the
animals that crawl on the earth'" (Genesis 1:28, BBE). So, from
the beginning, we were only *managers*, not *owners*, placed here
for *His* pleasure and glory, not our own. And this means that we
are managers for God even of our own lives because we did not
create ourselves and do not belong to ourselves. "Know that the
Lord [Jehovah], He is God. It is He Who has made us, and not
we ourselves. We are His people and the sheep in His care" (Psalm
100:3, NKJV/GW).

However, the corrupting and intoxicating idea that we could
become owners was first proposed by Satan in the form of the
serpent: "If you eat the forbidden fruit, then you shall be a god
yourself, knowing everything, including good and evil" (Genesis

3:1–7, paraphrase). Until this point, everything in Adam's and Eve's life had depended on God. He was the responsible party for their entire welfare because He was the God. But by biting the forbidden fruit, human beings replaced *Him* with *themselves*—and they have been choking on that bite ever since!

Why? Just what are the ramifications of being your own god? Immediately you take on the awful responsibility of maintaining your own life. Want to be happy? Then, if you are the god, you've got to make happiness happen yourself. Want to be secure? Then you've got to bring about your own security. Want to be significant and find meaning in your life? Then you, being the god, have got to find some kind of transcendent purpose for your existence. But being only a creature of finiteness rather than infiniteness, you simply don't know enough to make any of this happen. You barely understand the past, hardly know the significance of what's really happening in the present, and have absolutely no idea of what's happening in the future!

Yet everything in your life now depends on you, since *you* are the god. You have pushed the real God, the only truly *capable* God, out of your life and substituted your very incapable and limited self as the god. *The weight of your entire existence now rests solely on your own incredibly frail shoulders!* It becomes painfully clear almost immediately that you will be completely overwhelmed—no matter how hard you try or who you might be or how much you think you know, or how much money and clout you have. *You simply are not the man for the job.* You are a frail, finite, transient human being, but the job requires a God—a *real* God.

This is the fix we humans find ourselves in, *way* out of our league. We literally kill ourselves trying to live! We literally stress ourselves to death. Ultimately, we control absolutely nothing but worry ourselves crazy because we realize that without any control, we are in perpetual peril. And when this scary, awful reality gets too heavy for us, we anesthetize ourselves with drugs, alcohol, sex, pleasures, thrill-seeking, and various other means and methods to change our *perception* of this awful reality.

Finally—and this is why the message of Jesus Christ and the Gospel is such powerfully good news—we throw up both hands, first in despair, then in absolute surrender, and *beg* Him to take the load off our shoulders and run our unbelievably complex, miserable little lives for us. And Jesus has invited us to do just this in Matthew 11:28: "Come to me all of you who are tired from the heavy burden you have been forced to carry. I will give you rest" (ERV). "I will ease and relieve and refresh your souls" (AMP). Is there any better news to a person who has felt the weight of the whole world pressing them down?

Thus, radical submission is the way to put God back into His rightful place in your life. Only *He* is the God and the owner of your life. You are only the created being and the manager. *Submission removes the overwhelming, too-heavy-to-carry task of caring for yourself from your list of responsibilities and puts it all back on God, Who can easily handle it all.* "Cast all your cares upon Him and let Him do the caring for you" (1 Peter 5:7, paraphrased).

Let God be God, and you be His well-loved child. The difference is like night and day, unbelievable freedom versus soul-oppressive slavery!

QUESTIONS:

1. Do you see any areas in your life where you are still trying to take over for God and run the show?
2. What act on your part removes the task of managing and caring for yourself as though you have power to do so? Are you experiencing freedom as a result of this act on your part?
3. What goes into managing your life in a responsible manner for God?

PRAYER:

Oh, Lord, we are sorry for taking on a job that was entirely and utterly too big for us: trying to run our own show and be our own god. Forgive us for such presumption. You alone created the world and us, and You alone know how to keep it all going. Help us to trust in that fact—then relax and be happy. For Christ's sake, amen.

Lesson 22: Take Control of Your Peace of Mind Today

"And the harvest of righteousness (of conformity to God's will in thought and deed) is [the fruit of the seed] sown in peace by those who work for and make peace [in themselves and in others, that peace which means concord, agreement, and harmony between individuals, with undisturbedness, in a peaceful mind free from fears and agitating passions and moral conflicts]."

James 3:8 (AMP)

There are many ways to describe submission. Submission is character. Submission is self-discipline. Submission is self-control. *Submission is bringing everything in your life into conformity with the Word of God.* Submission is discipleship. Submission is making Jesus Christ Lord *of* all; otherwise, He is not lord *at* all. As the late Elisabeth Elliot has said, "Until the will and the affections are brought under the authority of Christ, we have not begun to understand, let alone to accept, His lordship."

Submission is doing what you ought to do even when you don't feel like doing it and even when the opportunity arises for you to do something else more pleasant. Submission is maintaining moral purity and integrity in an unbelievably morally corrupt world. Submission is refusing to indulge yourself in the sin and selfishness that this world gives you liberty to indulge in, but instead, you stay true to your convictions even while all the world and half the church is abusing its liberty in Christ (Galatians 5:13; 1 Peter 2:16; 1 Corinthians 6:12).

Submission is living life by strong, God-given convictions even when it might hurt you in some way. Submission is telling the truth even when the truth might get you into big financial trouble. For example, one Christian woman's daughter had a wreck in the family car. The woman told the insurance company that she herself was driving because the insurance company would not have paid if the daughter were driving. Furthermore, her husband would have been furious. Submission says to be honest even when it hurts.

Therefore, today, you must desperately take control of your own spiritual life. "Work out your own salvation with fear and trembling..." (Philippians 2:12, KJV). Pray, cry, fast, beg, do whatever is necessary to receive a greater revelation of His divine love for you so that you can completely submit yourself to God and gain victory in Christ. You do *not* want to be vulnerable to and under the control of circumstances, schemes of men, powers of hell, or such like.

A preacher once asked a man, "How are you doing today?"

The man replied, "Okay, under the circumstances."

So the preacher challenged him, "And what are you doing under *there*?"

Too many of us Christians are under the control of our circumstances. Our peace of mind and spiritual well-being depend too much on what is happening to us. We often live lives of frustration and crankiness because things are going against us, and we "are having a bad day." *But under radical submission, there is no such thing as a bad day!*

Your goal is to find peace of heart and mind because true peace is the fruit of submission and "conformity to God's will"—and submission *only* (James 3:17–18). So then, this gives us yet another way to describe submission: *Whatever brings real and lasting peace and joy to your heart and mind is submission.* Whatever brings or permits these other human feelings is not submission but a form of rebellion: anger, hatred, resentment, vengefulness, questionings, unbelief, unforgiveness, bitterness, worry, fear, nervousness, care, stress, pressure, impatience, unthankfulness, depression, cynicism, jealousy, envy, stubbornness, contentiousness, fighting, blaming God, dissatisfaction, longing for "forbidden fruit," and the like.

My wife and I were having a conversation once when our family was under great financial stress and duress. We had both "prayed and committed it all into God's hands." I did my best not to worry. Hey, I called myself a "spiritually deep" preacher; I knew worrying was un-Christlike and something I was *not* supposed to be doing!

"So, are you worried?" she asked me.

"'Course not!" I replied. "I'm a preacher."

"Well, do you have *peace?*" she queried further. And I was stumped; she had me there! I definitely did not have peace about the situation.

"No," I quietly replied. "I guess not."

"*Well, whatever is not peace is worry,*" she wisely pointed out.

So I had to go back and do some more earnest praying until I truly had peace.

You, too, can have a *"peace that passes all understanding"* (Philippians 4:7, KJV) if you want it—or you can remain forever plagued and tormented in some form of fear and rebellion. It's *your* choice all the way.

I'll Keep Holding On To Jesus

Verse 1:
When I started long ago to trust Jesus, I was seeking for security,
For I needed something steady to hold to, And something that
would hold to me.

Chorus:
I'll keep holding on to Jesus, For no other Friend so faithful
could be.
I'll keep holding on to Jesus, For I know He's holding on to me.

Verse 2:
Well, I'm learning every day now to trust Him, And I'm finding
really He's all I need.
Earthly gods can only fail and betray you, But my Jesus is a
Friend indeed.

Verse 3:
Yes, I put my all in all in Jesus, And I'm trusting in His grace all
the way.
In the shelter of His will I am resting, With a peace that's growing sweeter each day.

From *I'll Keep Holding On To Jesus,* by the Evening Light Gospel
Harmonizers

© ℗ 1980 Philip A Matthews
https://www.youtube.com/watch?v=N7OA2IVrlJk&list=PLguoVahXr-
j0k-JYEPhbWcZ5aQmkXuHNrN
[Purchase at https://www.amazon.com/dp/B00DU5B8MG/ref=dm_ws_tlw_trk1*]*

QUESTIONS:

1. Do you have peace in every area of your life? That is, are you undisturbed, and do you have a *"peaceful mind free from fears and agitating passions and moral conflicts"*?
2. How can you obtain and maintain this depth of peace?

PRAYER:

Father God, so many of Your children are in great need of the kind of perfect peace that You came to bring and died to give us. Help us take the steps necessary to truly experience the depths of this "peace that passes all understanding." This You included as one of the main components of the Kingdom of God: "For God's Kingdom is not a matter of eating and drinking, but of the righteousness, peace, and joy which the Holy Spirit gives" (Romans 14:17, Good News Bible). So, In Jesus' name, we ask You to bless us, O God, in this way, and to You, we give all the praise, glory, and worship. Amen.

CHAPTER FOUR
THE PRACTICAL SIGNIFICANCE OF RADICAL SUBMISSION

Lesson 23: Most Christians Don't Practice Radical Submission

"Just because something is technically legal doesn't mean that it's spiritually appropriate. If I went around doing whatever I thought I could get by with, I'd be a slave to my whims."

1 Corinthians 6:12 (The Message)

At the beginning of this book, I said that most Christians today seldom practice or even know much about radical submission to God. We have lots of "Christians" but few disciples. What proof do I have to support this assertion? Well, let's look at the life of the average Christian and contrast it with God's way.

For example, God says trust Me, but we trust ourselves much more. Jesus says, *"Take no thought for your life,"* but we literally spend—that is, pour out and waste—our lives worrying and struggling over earthly matters. Multitudes of us are depressed and unhappy with our lives, although Jesus died to bring us "joy in the Holy Ghost" (Romans 14:17, KJV), and we claim that "God is in control."

Contrary to His instructions in 1 Corinthians 7:31—"Those who are busy with worldly affairs must not be overly absorbed in them" (Norlie: The NT)—the world absorbs us: almost all of our time, our loyalty, and our spiritual, mental, emotional, physical, and financial strength. God says I own everything you possess, not just a tenth (tithe), but only 4 percent of Christians can even tithe that tenth. In fact, according to Empty Tomb, a Christian research group, in 2013, Christians gave only 2.3 percent of their incomes, the lowest figure since the Depression.

God says stay with the wife of your youth, but we divorce our spouses at a rate almost as high as the world's: Thirty-five percent of so-called "born-again" Christians have gone through a divorce, which is statistically identical to the thirty-five percent among non-born again adults. And even atheists and agnostics are only a bit worse: 37 percent. But the real shock, according to researcher George Barna, is that 90 percent of these "born agains" experienced that divorce *after* they accepted Christ, not before! Barna concludes: "It is unfortunate that so many people, regardless of their faith, experience a divorce, but especially unsettling to find that the faith commitment of so many born again individuals has not enabled them to strengthen and save their marriages."[4]

God says dress modestly and decently, but so many of us look like we are in competition with some sex idol movie star. We seem to be deliberately intent on revealing as much of our flesh as allowable, knowing all along that accentuating our sex appeal is an integral part of the *world's* beauty standards, not *God's*. We seem to be driven by the fear of not belonging.

We are free, called to liberty, but instructed *not* to use our liberty for an occasion to fulfill the lusts of the flesh. Therefore, our liberty is limited. "You, my brothers," the Apostle Paul says in Galatians 5:13, "were called to be free. But do not use your freedom to indulge the sinful nature" (NIV) or as "an… excuse for selfishness" (AMP). The Apostle Peter gave the same admonition: "Live like free men, only do not use your freedom as an excuse for doing wrong…" (1 Peter 2:16, Goodspeed). And in 1 Corinthians 6:12 (The Message), Paul writes, "Just because something is technically legal doesn't mean that it's spiritually appropriate. If I went around doing whatever I thought I could get by with, I'd be a slave to my whims."

However, most Christians violate this rule every day. We tend to reserve the right to be selfish, although Christ, our Pattern and Example, was very *selfless*. In general, we live under the control of our own fleshly desires, appetites, preferences, and secular ambitions. We worship loudly, and we testify boldly, we get happy and shout in church on Sunday, but we hold on to the privilege to direct our own lives and choose our own paths. We don't go out and kill people, but if anybody crosses us, millions of us reserve the right to "go off" on other people and even "cuss them out" if we feel like it. Then we reserve the right to nurse our grudges and hold on to resentment and bitterness for years. We never seem to identify with Jesus' words and attitude, "Father, forgive them, for they don't know what they're doing."

We won't outright steal (hopefully), but we justify cheating on our taxes, although both Jesus and Paul instructed us to *"give to Caesar what belongs to Caesar"* (Matthew 22:18–22, KJV) and *"pay taxes to whom taxes are due, and revenue to whom revenue is due"* (Romans 13:7, KJV). Thirty years ago, the Gallup Poll found that churchgoers were nearly as likely as the unchurched to cheat on their taxes.

Additionally, we reserve the right to overeat, to please our flesh, to develop and keep bad habits (sometimes that kill us, like smoking and overdrinking), to fulfill our desires for pleasure, to seek hard after riches, and to give ourselves completely to the American Dream, which is actually a nightmare from God's perspective.

The "American Nightmare" is to acquire lots of possessions then spend the rest of our lives in a never-ending "rat race" to pay for and protect them.

But God's dream life is that *all* of His children would use their freedom to concentrate on enjoying fellowship with Him, serving other people, and saving the lost to build up His kingdom. And there are entirely too many *millions* of Christians who are only marginally involved with any of these three eternal desires of God.

The whole situation can all be summarized with the words of Ronald J. Snider in the "Introduction" to *The Scandal of the Evangelical Conscience: Why Are Christians Living Just Like the Rest of the World?*: "What a tragedy for evangelicals to declare proudly that personal conversion and new birth in Christ are at the center of their faith and then to defy biblical moral standards by living almost as sinfully as their pagan neighbors." What an indictment!

QUESTIONS:

1. What are your comments on this assertion that if we do not follow biblical instructions on how to live our lives, then we are not being submissive to God?
2. Is my life filled to the brim with carnality in how I talk, my actions, my thoughts, and my very spirit? Or does it reflect the Christ Who owns my life?

PRAYER:

Heavenly Father, as you look down on us all today, we need you to help us bring every thought, every deed, every attitude, and everything else in our lives into the "obedience of Christ" (2 Corinthians 10:5, KJV). For Christ's sake, amen.

Lesson 24: Christians Today Reserve the Right to Sin

"But don't let sin control your life here on earth. You must not be ruled by the things your sinful self makes you want to do. Don't offer the parts of your body to serve sin. Don't use your bodies to do evil, but offer yourselves to God, as people who have died and now live. Offer the parts of your body to God to be used for doing good."

Romans 6:12–13 (Easy-to-Read Version)

In the last lesson, we gave several examples of how millions of Christians reserve certain areas of their lives to selfishly do their own thing instead of submitting those areas to God and living in obedience to Him. But most of all, we reserve the right to sin. We reserve the right to harbor spiritual and mental impurity, to hold on to our selfishness, to cling to our fleshly natures. We actually fall in love with and cherish our selfishness and don't really want to give it up for all the world. We *enjoy* our sins, especially our secret sins. Really, just how willing are we to simply lose our privilege to do, say, and think the wrong things?

We *say* that we want to be absolutely pure inside, but just how strong is that desire, and how desperately convicted can we be when we know that God is willing to pardon us over and over and over again? We excuse and justify our impurity by claiming that the blood covers our sins—which is true. But when is the blood ever going to *cleanse* us from our sins so that we don't commit them anymore? Is there no longer such a thing as victory *over* sin? When are we going to be *transformed* and start living like Jesus? Whatever happened to holiness, i.e., true holy living that is *different* from the world?

The Bible—Old and New Testaments—is crammed full of scriptures that talk about sin being cleansed and our hearts, minds, and lives being made pure and righteous. But we can experience such only if we really choose to *give up* those sins. Being a Christian once meant having exemplary behavior, selfless motives, clean thoughts and desires, God-like love, and trustworthy character. Now it just means that "God's still working on me," so, in the meantime, nobody should expect me to behave any different than a non-Christian.

This was never quite the way God wanted things to go. And millions of Christians in the past sang about a different kind of victory in their lives:

Power in the Blood
By Lewis E Jones

Would you be free from your burden of sin? There's power in the blood, power in the blood;
Would you over evil a victory win? There's wonderful power in the blood.

Would you be free from your passion and pride? There's power in the blood, power in the blood;
Come for a cleansing to Calvary's tide, There's wonderful power in the blood...

Chorus: There is power, power, wonder-working power In the blood of the Lamb...

Or listen to another great hymn:

Glorious Freedom
By Haldor Lillenas

Once I was bound by sin's galling fetters, chained like a slave I
struggled in vain.
But I received Thy glorious freedom when Jesus broke my fetters in twain.

Chorus: Glorious freedom! Wonderful freedom! No more in chains
of sin I repine!
Jesus, the glorious Emancipator, now and forever, He shall be mine!

Freedom from all the carnal affections, freedom from envy,
hatred, and strife,
Freedom from vain and worldly ambition, freedom from all that
saddened my life.

Freedom from pride and all sinful follies, freedom from love
and glitter gold,
Freedom from evil temper and anger, glorious freedom, rap-
ture untold!

Freedom from fear with all of its torments, freedom from care
with all of its pain,
Freedom in Christ, my blessed Redeemer, He who has rent my
fetters in twain.

The average Christian's life is filled to the brim with carnality
in word, deed, thought, and spirit. Very little has been brought
into the "*captivity of Christ*" (2 Corinthians, 10:5). Some of our
most famous proponents live lives of such luxury that not only

would Jesus Christ never condone or participate in such a lifestyle, He would be utterly embarrassed by it. And He would be forced to disassociate Himself from such lifestyles.

This is because eternal things were His utmost concern, and earthly blessings were not even one of His goals for Himself or His disciples. And He, Who humbly entered the world as a pauper and lived His life as a servant, would find it completely against everything He stood for to allow Himself to be served and waited on and fawned upon as some kind of great earthly potentate.

Paul instructed: "But immorality (sexual vice) and all impurity [of lustful, rich, wasteful living] or greediness must not even be named among you, as is fitting and proper among saints (God's consecrated people)" (Ephesians 5:3, AMP).

But this kind of victory doesn't happen by chance, but by deliberately submitting to God and giving up your right to love and cling to your sins.

To many of us, radical submission to God is an unheard-of, unimaginable concept. Yet only perfect submission to God will prevent us from abusing our spiritual liberty. In every area of life where we are not perfectly submitted to God, we will *automatically* fulfill the lusts of our flesh. *If we don't bring everything in our lives under the Lordship of Jesus Christ, then, by default, it remains under the control of our own fleshly desires and therefore easily manipulated by Satan.*

Thus, radical submission will make a radical difference between your life and the lives of other, ordinary, selfishness-driven Christians.

QUESTIONS:

1. Discuss: Do you truly believe it's even possible for a person to overcome their bad habits that cause them to sin daily in thought, word, deed?
2. What is your plan to finally overcome the sins that you have wrestled with for years?

PRAYER:

Oh, Lord, we have reached a time where *"sin abounds,"* but we know that Your *"grace does much more abound"* (Romans 5:20, KJV). So, we refuse to submit to You, and instead, we settle for spiritual weakness and crippled testimonies. Help us to begin to overcome our "besetting sins" (Hebrews 12:1), one by one. Make us men and women of greater conviction and help us to desire to win these battles with and against ourselves. Motivate us to victory, In Jesus' name, amen.

Lesson 25: Very Few Christians Have a Biblical Worldview

"Remember that there will be difficult times in the last days. People will be selfish, greedy, boastful, and conceited; they will be insulting, disobedient to their parents, ungrateful, and irreligious; they will be unkind, merciless, slanderers, violent, and fierce; they will hate the good; they will be treacherous, reckless, and swollen with pride; they will love pleasure rather than God; they will hold to the outward form of our religion, but reject its real power. Keep away from such people."

2 Timothy 3:1–5 (Good News Bible)

This is almost a perfect description of modern people today. *"They love pleasure more than they love God."* But perhaps the biggest shock in this passage is that, no matter how evil people become, they still claim some form of religion! So, in the end, this becomes a description of religious people, including many "Christians," not just secular, non-Christian people. They "believe," but "their conduct belies the genuineness of their profession" (AMP). They claim to be "Christian," but "they refuse to let that 'devotion' change the way they live" (ERV).

Probably the best supporting evidence for the assertion that most Christians do not live lives of submission to God is found in George Barna's research of Christians' worldviews. In March 2020, he found that while 70 percent of all Americans consider themselves to be Christian, only 6 percent of them have a biblical worldview as the basis for their attitudes, beliefs, values, opinions, and behavior![5]

More alarming was his finding that only 19 percent of *born-again Christians,* the supposedly "cream of the crop" Christians, have a biblical worldview! Breaking it down by religious classifications, he found these proportions of adults possessed a biblical worldview: Mainline Protestant churches (8 percent), Evangelical Protestant churches (21 percent), Pentecostal churches (16 percent), Baptist churches (8 percent), and Catholics (less than 1 percent).[6] So obviously, this troubling condition seems to plague most churches to a very great degree!

Exactly what is a biblical worldview? A biblical worldview is defined to possess these eight critical beliefs that are clearly and indisputably taught by the Bible:

1. Absolute moral truths exist, so right and wrong are *not* relative;
2. Such truth is defined by the Bible;
3. Jesus Christ lived a sinless life;
4. The God of the Bible is the all-powerful and all-knowing Creator of the universe and He still rules it today;
5. Salvation is a gift from God and cannot be earned;
6. Satan is a real being, not merely a *symbol* of evil;
7. Christians have the responsibility to share their faith in Christ with other people; and
8. The Bible is accurate in *all* of its teachings.

At first glance, it would appear that few Christians would disagree with any of these critical beliefs, but finding Christians who firmly believe all eight of these foundational convictions is a rarity, as stated in the stats above.

Indeed, finding *pastors* who believe and *teach their people* all eight of these truths is not too common: Barna found that only 51 percent of Protestant pastors have a biblical worldview. By gender, 53 percent of male pastors have a biblical worldview, but only 15 percent of female pastors believe so. By ethnicity, 55 percent of white pastors and 30 percent of black pastors ascribe to a biblical worldview.[7] So, if the leaders themselves don't ascribe to a biblical worldview, is there any wonder that their parishioners don't?

Instead, most Christians have a postmodern worldview, which believes that there is no such thing as absolute moral truth. Many do not use God's Word when making most of their daily decisions of life but instead use a pragmatic approach in which the end justifies the means. That is, "If it works, let's do it." Whether or not it's morally right or biblically taught seldom seems to enter the picture.

For example, 70 percent of women who have had abortions call themselves "Christian," and 75 percent of those say that their church had no influence at all in their decision to abort their babies! This is according to a November 2015 survey conducted by LifeWay Research, associated with the Southern Baptist Convention, and sponsored by the Care Net network of anti-abortion pregnancy centers: http://www.charismanews.com/culture/53499-70-percent-of-women-who-have-had-abortions-call-themselves-christians.

Now, this is how our worldview affects our submission to God and our behavior: *A person's worldview determines his moral behavior. A person who does not have a biblical worldview will not submit to live his life in radical obedience to God's Word because he does not really believe or accept all of God's Word as true and absolute.*

Thus, Barna found these contrasts in the behaviors of those who have a biblical worldview (first stat in each pair below) and those who do not have a biblical worldview (second stat in each pair). The biblical worldview-ers were:

1. 31 times less likely to regard cohabitation as morally acceptable (2 percent vs. 62 percent);
2. 18 times less likely to endorse drunkenness (2 percent vs. 36 percent);
3. 15 times less likely to condone gay sex (2 percent vs. 31 percent);
4. 11 times less likely to describe adultery as morally acceptable (4 percent vs. 44 percent) and 25 times less likely to have committed adultery in the last month (less than 1 percent vs. 12 ½ percent);
5. 78 times less likely to approve of pornography (less than one-half of 1 percent vs. 39 percent);
6. 12 times less likely to accept profanity (3 percent vs. 37 percent);
7. 92 times less likely to endorse abortion (less than one-half of 1 percent vs. 46 percent); and
8. 8 to 17 times less likely to buy lottery tickets or gamble.
9. Also, biblical worldview-ers were twice as likely to have discussed spiritual matters with others recently and twice as likely to have fasted for religious reasons in the past month.[8]

Obviously, Christians who hold to a biblical worldview possess *radically* different views on morality, hold greatly divergent religious beliefs closer to the true intent of the Bible, and demonstrate vastly different lifestyle choices and behavior. True submission to God requires a person to daily live his or her life from a biblical worldview. Knowingly refusing or neglecting to do so is only another form of spiritual rebellion.

QUESTIONS:

1. Discuss: Based on the spiritual signs Paul left in 2 Timothy 3:1–5, do you believe that we are in the "last days"?
2. What is *your* plan to avoid becoming one of these religious hypocrites who "will appear to have a godly life, but they will not let its power change them" (2 Timothy 3:5, GW)? Jesus predicted in Matthew 24:12 that "there will be so much more evil in the world that the love of most believers will grow cold" (ERV). How will that not happen to you?
3. Do I use God's Word when making my daily decisions in Life?

PRAYER:

Father God, as we see the Day so quickly approaching, please protect our hearts from falling out of love with You and falling in love with this dying society. Help us to realize that when we neglect to know Your Word or refuse to obey its principles, we open our lives up to be victimized by the many deceptions floating around in this world. Help us to know the Truth, believe the Truth, live by the Truth, and be set free by the Truth. In Jesus' mighty name, amen.

Lesson 26: Submission Brings Divine Order into Our Lives

"He sent His Word and healed them, and delivered them from their destructions."

Psalm 107:20 (KJV)

Some Christians spend too much time and effort "rebuking the devil" or seeking some spiritual "high" when all the time, what we really need to do is bring everything in our lives into the order of the Lord. Indeed, depending on weekly, church-induced, warm, fuzzy feelings or ecstatic experiences to drown out the unhappiness and problems we have brought upon ourselves is hardly any different than anesthetizing ourselves with alcohol.

Yet every Sunday, there are thousands of people shouting in church, lifting "holy hands" and singing "no weapon formed against me shall prosper," when all along they're living with their fourth wife or somebody else they're not even married to at all. Or they're using dishonest business practices or visiting Internet porn sites. Or they're making a million other spiritual compromises, their lives filled with unscriptural conditions. Very few of them are really *"fitting themselves into His plans"* (Romans 8:28, TLB). Instead, many of them are trying to fit *God* into *their* plans. Yet, they seem to think that church is going to fix it all or that some spiritual zapping or magic prayer is going to help them avoid the consequences of their rebellious choices.

Jude exhorted us to *"guard and keep yourselves in [or in step with] the love of God..."* (Jude 21, CEV and AMP). The Greek word, *tereo*, means to "keep from escaping." Jesus Himself had taught earlier that *"If you keep My commandments, you will abide and live in My love"* (John 15:10, KJV). *To get God's blessings in your life, you must make decisions that stay within the guidelines and constraints in God's Word.* Otherwise, Galatians 6:7–8 (TLB) will apply: "Don't be misled; remember that you can't ignore God and get away with it: a man will always reap just the kind of crop he sows! If he sows to please his own wrong desires, he will be planting seeds of evil and he will surely reap a harvest of spiritual decay and death; but if he plants the good things of the Spirit, he will reap the everlasting life which the Holy Spirit gives him." There is just no way to avoid the consequences of your own selfish decisions.

The Psalmist wrote, "Order my steps by Your Word, that is, let my steps be guided by your word; and let not sin have control over me" (Psalm 119:133, KJV/BBE). In other words, let You, oh Lord, be the One guiding and controlling my moves, and don't let iniquity, i.e., my own willfulness, be in control. The motto of every church we have planted has always been, "There is no problem on earth that the Word of God, rightly applied, cannot either remedy or prevent." *Submission to God's Word in every area of life heals and brings divine order into your life.*

You don't always need some kind of miraculous deliverance if you submit to live by God's principles of life to start with. If you are a sheep and you stay in the pasture where God has ordained and provided special built-in protections for His sheep, then truly "no weapon formed against you shall prosper" (Isaiah 54:17, KJV). But if you start wandering all out in the spiritual wilderness, refusing to live by His principles of life while you do your own thing and follow the trends and values of this world, then the devil has a whole world of weapons formed against you, tailor-made and customized just for you, that will definitely bring destruction and misery into your life. And loud, enthusiastic singing in church won't prevent it!

There can very well be a such thing as a "generational curse," but what many Christians are calling "generational curses" are often nothing more than the awful consequences of refusing to live life in submission to God and His Word.

I'll use myself as an example. Once I went into a church for prayer and mentioned that I had borderline high blood pressure. The minister started praying about a "generational curse." Actually, I've known all my life that this tendency for high blood pressure was passed down from previous generations to me on my genes as a baby. My grandmother died from it before I was born.

But having it on my genes was not the end of the matter. Like most Americans, I spent my first four decades limitlessly indulging my appetite for all the richest, greasiest, saltiest foods, overeating, neglecting to exercise, gaining weight, losing sleep, stressing myself out every day in the rat race. You know, the average American diet and lifestyle. Then, as I neared fifty years old, I discovered that the "generational curse" had at last hit me—I had borderline high blood pressure and had to start watching my diet like an old man—and the church is ready to rebuke it in Jesus' name.

God can definitely heal me, but what I really need to recognize is that my real problem was not some "generational curse," but my lifelong habit of refusing to submit myself to God's principles of sober and sensible living regarding my diet. It wasn't my grandmother who brought this disease upon me; it was my own lack of self-control. We must submit to God in the way we treat our own bodies.

Thus, the first answer for the "curse of sin" is to bring everything in our lives under radical submission to God. Only then can the "curse of sin" no longer afflict our lives. For example, I might be saved, and my wife might be saved, but if we don't operate our family and raise our children according to the principles of the Word of God, the curse of sin will continue to negatively affect our lives and our children's lives—no matter that we are praise-singing, devil-rebuking Christians. Your children reflect *your* choices, not their ancient ancestors'.

Looking around at the Christian world, we see far too many Christian lives and families cursed and full of self-induced troubles. Jesus Christ paid an awful price to bring us infinite blessings and escape from the consequences of the corruption afflicting all human beings (2 Peter 1:2–4). But the power that enables us to fully receive the benefits of having the "curse of sin" broken in our lives is radical submission to God and to the authority of His Word.

What I have found is that most people, including most Christians, really do not want to live a life of submission. They really just want to enjoy God's blessings and benefits without completely letting Him rule their lives. They want Him to get them out of the fixes they have gotten themselves into, but they don't want to let Him tell them how not to get into any more fixes. They want Him to remove their depression without allowing Him the privilege of removing the unscriptural attitudes, actions, and other stuff in their lives that are causing or fueling that depression.

They don't want Him or anybody else telling them what to do in the details of their lives, and the moment certain subjects are broached, they start screaming, "Legalism! I'm saved by grace! I'm free in the Spirit!" But the truth is that a life of absolute submission to God emphasizes *temperance* (self-control—Acts 24:25; Galatians 5:23 a "fruit of the Spirit"), *self-crucifixion of the flesh* (Galatians 5:24), *separation from the world* (John 17:14–16; 1 John 2:15–17; James 4:4), and *the practice of love and forgiveness* in all—even difficult—situations and relationships (1 Corinthians 13:1–7). And these are the areas in which millions of us so-called spiritually "free" Christians have difficulty being consistently Christ-like.

QUESTIONS:

1. In what ways would you admit to "abusing your spiritual freedom?"
2. Identify where you need improvement in your living according to God's principles of life. Consider the following areas: personal devotion, reflection, and meditation time; time management; nutrition/eating habits; anger management; neighbor and personal outreach; maintaining healthy relationships; and financial affairs.

PRAYER:

Oh, Jesus, help us know Your Word, believe and accept Your Word as always true, and obey Your Word in submission to You. Keep us from searching for some other easier, more desirable way. Help us to remember that "There is a way that seems right to a person, but eventually it ends in death" (Proverbs 16:25, GW). In Your Blessed Name, amen.

Lesson 27: Most People Are Mortally Wounded

*"The Spirit of the Almighty LORD is with me because the LORD
has anointed me to deliver good news to humble people. He has
sent me to heal those who are brokenhearted, to announce that
captives will be set free and prisoners will be released."*

Isaiah 61:1 (God's Word)

It doesn't take long to realize that this world is chock full of hurting,
wounded people. Almost everybody seems to exhibit symptoms
and signs of woundedness. So, we move into the church and expect
to find different people—emotionally and spiritually healthier
folks. Instead, we find a great incidence of wounded Christians
with compulsive behaviors, driven by fear:

> Christians who cannot trust or obey God because of fear.
> Workaholic Christians who can never allow themselves to
> relax because busyness makes them feel important. Perfec-
> tionist Christians who can never be pleased with themselves
> or anybody else. Christian addicts who cannot quit smoking,
> eating, drinking, shopping, gambling, and indulging in other
> compulsions that are gradually destroying them. Christians
> who cannot quit seeking for affirmation and acceptance from
> the opposite sex, sometimes even though they are married
> and must pursue these relationships illicitly. Others who seem
> addicted to constantly having a romantic relationship going
> at all times simply because they get their feelings of security,
> significance, and approval from such relationships.

We have millions of Christians who have no control over their emotions. Christians who are so sensitive and whose feelings are so easily hurt that others must handle them with "kid gloves." Some get their feelings hurt if you merely look at them the wrong way or forget to speak to them at church. Others spend most of their lives pouting and seething and thinking negative thoughts. We have millions of Christians who cannot trust anybody but are suspicious of everybody, even God. Christians who are driven to dominate, control, manipulate, and abuse others for their own selfish, emotional purposes and dishonest, ulterior motives. Feminist Christians and other militant Christians who seem obsessed with fighting for their rights and combating perceived social insults and injustices. Depressed Christians who know absolutely nothing about the *"peace of God which passes all understanding."*

There are countless millions of Christians whose lives are controlled by jealousy, bitterness, self-protection, revenge, disrespect, rebellion, pride, putting down others, and all the other symptoms of woundedness. Christians who are ruled by compulsive talkativeness, constant clowning to attract attention, timidity, and other manifestations of insecurity. Christians whose lives are plagued by cynicism and unbelief instead of hope and faith. Christians who are seriously thinking about killing themselves—and many who actually do. Even Christian ministers who use their ministries mostly to derive their self-worth and emotional and spiritual security from *God's* work and *God's* gifts.

Granted, not *all* Christians are like this. *But still, the Christian world is literally filled to overflowing with such hurting, wound-driven Christians. Internal emotional bleeding characterizes this age and this church.*

Thus, the greatest need of our age is the need for spiritual healing. Scarred and wounded people inevitably hurt and scar other people—their children, their wives, their husbands, their friends, and their society as a whole. Their behavior and character traits damage everyone who touches their lives. One selfish generation just passes down their hurts and brokenness to the next selfish generation, ad infinitum, keeping the vicious cycle going from the time of Adam and Eve to the end of time. Something and somebody needs to stop this craziness. Jesus Christ came to do this, but it "just ain't happening!" Without spiritual healing, life is not truly happy. Real contentment, satisfaction, and freedom from fear and anxiety remain very elusive. Wholeness and whole people are increasingly rare in the church.

Of course, this is not the way God intended for things to be. This is subpar Christianity, and some may not be true Christians at all. For this reason, one of Jesus' first messages, recorded in Luke 4:18–19 (KJV), is a quote of Isaiah 61:1–3 (KJV): "The Spirit of the Lord is upon Me, because He has anointed Me to preach the gospel to the poor. He has sent Me to heal the brokenhearted, to preach deliverance to the captives and recovering of sight to the blind, to set at liberty those who are bruised [and crushed and oppressed—AMP], to preach the acceptable year of the Lord."

Obviously, from this text, we can clearly see that God wants to heal us. Indeed, until He does heal us, not only will our lives be filled with misery, but we will not be able to obey Him. We will not be very successful in serving Him. *We cannot possibly do what He, by His Spirit or His Word, tells us to do if we are still under the bondage of doing what our old wounds tell us to do.*

Therefore, we must be healed, freed, and delivered to truly please God with our lives. God had this in mind when He sent Jesus into this world. His goal and desires were not merely forgiveness of our sins but complete spiritual healing and restoration. He wants us to experience being *whole* in every way.

Healing—spiritual, emotional, mental, physical, and social—is in His atonement: "He was wounded for our transgressions, He was bruised for our iniquities; the chastisement for our peace was upon Him, and with his stripes we are healed" (Isaiah 53:5 KJV). "He sent His Word and healed them, and delivered them from their destructions" (Psalm 107:20, KJV). Yet, most people spend their lives trying to hide and *compensate* for their wounds and insecurities instead of getting *healed and being made whole*. We spend untold amounts of time, effort, and money desperately trying to soothe the headache and mask the pain instead of curing the disease.

But through radical submission to God, true healing and restoration can take place.

QUESTIONS:

1. Reflect upon the areas that you know of where you are in need of divine "healing."

PRAYER:

Lord, we are so very thankful that You came to bring healing because *all* of us have been wounded. Most of us are *still* wounded in some way. So, as we take time to focus on our healing, reveal to us clearly the areas of woundedness and formulate a path to healing. Let each of us pray as David prayed: "Investigate my life, O God, find out everything about me; Cross-examine and test me, get a clear picture of what I'm about..." (Psalm 139:23, The Message). Then lead us in the way that brings more relief from pain, more spiritual and emotional victories, and more abundant, eternal life. In Jesus' name, amen.

Lesson 28: Radical Submission Heals

"Who his own self bore our sins in his own body on the tree, that we, being dead to sins, should live unto righteousness: by whose stripes ye were healed."

1 Peter 2:24 (KJV)

There are four critical steps to true spiritual healing and recovery:

Step 1—Recognize and admit your woundedness, i.e., admit that you have a problem. Do not minimize it. If you have any traits similar to those mentioned above or elsewhere in this book, admit that you have those weaknesses and resolve that you are going to be healed and *"out of weakness, be made strong"* (Hebrews 11:34, KJV). Don't excuse this woundedness just because everybody else acts the same way, and it's "just human." *That's simply because the "normal" human being is one big gaping sore!* The "average" man (or woman) is badly broken, just a "piece of a man." But Jesus died to lift you above what's normal and average. "Confess your faults to one another and pray for one another, so that you may be healed" (James 5:16, KJV).

Step 2—Quit blaming others, God, circumstances, etc. *You* have the problem, even if it originated from something somebody else did or said. But now it's about what *you* are going to do about it *now.* So somebody said something harsh to you this morning, and you "went off" on them because it's their fault. But really, it wasn't what she said that caused your bad reaction. Instead, it was *your own lack of wholeness*. A whole person like Jesus wouldn't have reacted that way (see Matthew 5:44). A whole person like Jesus would have returned love for that person's bad treatment or harsh words. He would have realized that people who hurt others are actually very hurt people themselves, and He would have loved them like God loves all of us wounded souls. *So, ask God to show you what you have lying beneath that symptom and that reaction you demonstrated—and He will. Then start working on* you!

Step 3—Forgive everything and everybody. Forgive God, Who allowed this thing to happen in the first place. Forgive the people who hurt you because weak hurting people hurt other people automatically. So you couldn't have and shouldn't have expected anything better from them. "They know not what they do," Jesus said of the people nailing Him to the cross (Luke 23:34, KJV). Forgive society, circumstances, fate, or whoever, whatever, wherever. Jesus Christ was so whole that He actually forgave people *before* they offended Him! (See John 19:11, KJV.) As Alan Paton, a South African author, and anti-apartheid activist, said, "There is a hard law... When an injury is done to us, *we* never recover until we forgive."

Step 4—Submit to God: Everything in your life is first filtered by God before it even comes to you:

- He won't let you suffer more than you can bear: "God is faithful, and he will not allow you to be tempted beyond your strength. Instead, along with the temptation, he will also provide a way out, so that you may be able to endure it" (1 Corinthians 10:13, ISV).

- Nothing is out of His control or escapes His notice: "Not even a sparrow falls to the ground without your Father noticing it" (Matthew 10:29, AMP).

- His love for you is infinite: "I've never quit loving you and never will. Expect love, love, and more love!" (Jeremiah 31:3, The Message).

- "He will perfect everything concerning you" (Psalm 138:8, KJV).

- No one has any power over you unless He permits it: "You meant evil against me, but God meant it for good" (Genesis 50:20, NASB) and "You would not have any power or authority whatsoever against (over) Me if it were not given you from above," Jesus told Pilate (John 19:11, AMP).

- "And we know that *all* that happens to us is working for our good *if* we love God and are fitting into His plans" (Romans 8:28, TLB).

- "Entrust (commit) your ways to the LORD. Trust him, and He will act on your behalf" (Psalm 37:5, GW). "... He'll do whatever needs to be done" (Message).

God can *be trusted! So submit everything into His control.* It's already in His control, but you need to release it from your own control— *especially since you don't really have any control anyway!* "*Let go and let God!*" This is the way to healing, wholeness, and abundant life.

"Take Me" by J Moss on V4... The Other Side of Victory
(http://www.youtube.com/watch?v=Cr_nyLYtI54&feature=player_embedded)

I dig into myself and I see hurt, I dig a little deeper and I see pain,
I see myself as an average person.
I dig into myself and I see the rain, I'm looking for a way to
make it dissipate,

I'm tired of crying and I hope it doesn't worsen.

Does He really care for me? Does He really know anything
about me?
Does He really hold the world in His hands? Is He too big that
He couldn't understand?
Is He too far away that He can't hear what I need Him to hear?
I need Him to be near.

Chorus:
Have I gone too far away from Your presence? Oh, my God, I'm
running back to you.
Have I strayed away, too far to hear what You say? Oh, my God,
I'm coming back to You.
Take me, take me…

I look up into my eyes and I see tears, I do some soul-searching
and I see fear.
I see myself as an injured person.
I try to keep safe from the struggle and the storm, but try to
find a way to make it move on,
I don't want this discouragement to worsen, yeah.

Does He really care for me? Does He really know anything
about me…

Inner Healing
Perhaps something should be said concerning the relationship
between inner healing ministry and radical submission. Many times,
a person may have wounds from the past that are extremely difficult
to deal with or even to remember. There needs to be a healing of
memories, emotions, and personality traits that are acquired because
of those wounds. There needs to be a more intimate revelation and

experience of God's love. Also, a relearning of patterns of behavior needs to occur. Because time does not always—or usually—heal many of these issues, special counseling is often required to dig down into these memories to uncover the hidden hurts, the unmet needs, the deceptive lies that have been accepted and believed, and the repressed emotions that prevent a person from getting to the truth which can set them free (John 8:32).

Thus, inner healing becomes a tool to achieve this. Although there are many different methods and names for the process of inner healing, it basically consists of three parts: counseling, interactive healing prayer, and practical follow-up. (1) Counseling, as described above, gives a person insight into issues they might not be able to discover on their own. (2) Conversational healing prayer enables a person to visualize the specific situation in the past where the hurt occurred, allows the Holy Spirit to walk through it with them, then reveals the truth and ministers the love to the person that was needed when the event first took place. Healing prayer is the miraculous and supernatural aspect of the inner healing process. (3) Finally, once the person has been freed from the pain and compulsions of the hurts, practical follow-up creates disciplines and routines to be practiced so that their outward patterns of life reflect the inner growth and healing achieved.

Radical submission kicks in during the conversational prayer part of the process. During prayer, God supernaturally reveals many things to the person, which requires forgiveness, letting go, renunciation of bitterness and resentment, self-denial, willingness to love through adversity, renunciation of the use of non-God solutions (e.g., hypnotism, witchcraft, the occult, and such), etc. All of these are forms of submission to God. So, it can be said that inner healing is a means to reveal what a person needs to do in order to be restored to emotional and spiritual health, and radical submission is *being willing* to do those things and then actually doing them. Through inner healing, God shows you who you are and how much He really loves you. By radical submission, you actually start trusting Him because you are experiencing that love. Through inner healing, God shows you *who* to forgive and *how* to forgive. By radical submission, you actually let go and release the offenders. The two go hand in hand.

Further reading/resources regarding inner healing:
Inner Healing—Transformation (formerly Theophostic) Prayer Ministry (TPM):
https://www.transformationprayer.org/.

Healing of Memories, David A Seamands, ISBN: 0-89693-532-9.
http://www.amazon.com/Healing-Memories-David-Seamands/dp/0896935329/ref=sr_1_1?s=books&ie=UTF8&qid=1393315312&sr=1-1&keywords=healing+of+memories.

How to Pray for Inner Healing for Yourself and Others, Rita Bennett, ISBN: 0-8007-5126-4.
http://www.amazon.com/Pray-Inner-Healing-Yourself-Others/dp/0800751264/ref=sr_1_1?ie=UTF8&qid=1461555239&sr=8-1&keywords=how+to+pray+-for+inner+healing+for+yourself.

1. Ask yourself this question: "Can I trust God about my wounds, now that I know and understand much more about what it means to engage in a humble and submissive relationship with Him?"
2. Which of the above four steps do you find most difficult to do?

PRAYER:

Heaven Father, I am convinced of Your unconditional love for me. Therefore, I am more than ready to experience Your healing touch in those secret, highly protected areas of my heart. I open up my heart to You. I relinquish the sensitivities that I have held on to so tightly. I reject the lies that spring from my woundedness and accept the Truth of Your infinite love. *In fact, I now see that the moment-by-moment awareness of Your infinite love is the definition of healing.* I am ready to see the works of the devil permanently destroyed in my life by Your blood spilled on the Cross—for *me and my healing*! I ask forgiveness for not forgiving You and others and for not trusting You. Heal me, renew me, rebuild me, and help me move forward in victory and wholeness from this day on. Thank You in the name of Jesus, my Savior, amen.

Lesson 29: Radical Submission Is Not Optional

"Refusing to obey is as bad as the sin of sorcery. Being stubborn and doing what you want is like the sin of worshiping idols."

1 Samuel 15:23 (ERV)

Now, if, as a submitted Christian, you have vowed to God that everything you have is His and you will no longer be in control of your own life, then any disobedience should be viewed as the serious act of rebellion that it really is. Disobedience can no longer be taken as lightly as it is so commonly taken today. "I failed to do what I promised God I would do, but so what? I refused to do what He told me to do, but so what? He loves me anyway, and He overlooks everything anyway, and He hardly cares because my sins are under the blood anyway," etc.

The hard truth of the matter is that the opposite of submission is rebellion. And God, contrary to popular belief, does not overlook and excuse rebellion. We Christians need to quit fooling ourselves. *"Rebellion,"* Samuel told a disobedient King Saul, "is as the sin of witchcraft, and stubbornness is as iniquity and idolatry" (1 Samuel 15:23, KJV).

This is no small, inconsequential matter. This is major trouble—big league stuff—as far as God is concerned, up there with idolatry, worshiping another god! Actually, He hates it. It's not something He really likes to tolerate, although He may be patient and longsuffering with us. But we Christians ought to be more concerned about how we view disobedience. *A persistent lack of submission to the divine can and will break fellowship with the divine Father. And the blood of Jesus does not atone for people who choose to remain in rebellion against and out of fellowship with God! Don't fool yourself!*

Look at it this way: When Jesus, in the Garden of Gethsemane, was struggling as a mere man to reaffirm His submission to the divine will, what really were His options? To simply tell the Father, "I just can't do it, Dad. It will hurt too bad. It'll go against my plans; I'm sorry about Yours. I really want to hang around a little longer. Spend some more quality time with Mary and Martha. Maybe next time, Dad. At least I tried."

Such would have been the height of rebellion, no less serious than the rebellion of Satan. And the damnation would have been no less than the damnation Satan is under. The message? *We don't really have any safe, acceptable alternatives to radical submission to God's will!*

So, for the Christian, perfect submission is *not* optional, although that is entirely how most of us live. We are happy and satisfied as long as we can say, "At least I'm saved." Many of us even add, "I'm glad I'm saved and sanctified" or "I'm saved and baptized with the Holy Ghost." Others go around mistakenly thinking that once they are saved, they are saved forever, no matter what they do or how rebelliously they act thereafter.

But your *initial* salvation is not necessarily your *final* salvation; otherwise, Peter would never have admonished the Christian to *"make your calling and election* sure" (2 Peter 1:10, KJV). Continual submission to God is necessary for continual fellowship with Him.

God saved you so that He could possess you and control your life. If you do not allow Him to possess and control your life, if you knowingly reserve certain areas for yourself and shut Him out, then how can that be anything other than the spirit of rebellion?

Unless we perfectly submit to God's will, we are still in a degree of rebellion, the same kind of rebellion that plunged the world into sin back in the Garden of Eden. *A little rebellion goes an awfully long way!* Eve was merely trying to find a way to live her life without absolute dependence on God, without complete submission to His will. She didn't commit adultery, she wasn't a prostitute or a dope dealer, nor did she murder anybody.

All she did was eat a harmless little piece of fruit! She did not dislike God; she was not super dissatisfied with her life; she was not a serial rapist or an armed robber. She only wanted what every human being wants: The chance to control his or her own life just a little bit, independently of God. *Sin is not found merely in the dastardliness of the deed you do but in the rebellious attitude and condition of heart that keeps you from submitting completely to God.*

Thus, Christians can be saved (forgiven) and remain in a state of partial rebellion, merely by refusing or neglecting to let God have absolute sway in their lives. *"Have Thine Own way, Lord, Have Thine Own way; Have o'er my being absolute sway…"*

Do you know someone who has not quite given God that privilege completely? Then you know someone who is still in partial rebellion toward God. Do you know anyone who is really giving God the privilege of possessing them that completely? Then you know someone who is being used by God supernaturally.

The famous evangelist, D. L. Moody, was to have a campaign in England. An elderly pastor, one of the organizers, protested, "Why do we need this 'Mr. Moody?' He's uneducated and inexperienced. Who does he think he is anyway? Does he think he has a monopoly on the Holy Spirit?" A younger pastor replied, "No,

Mr. Moody does not have a monopoly on the Holy Spirit, but the Holy Spirit certainly has a monopoly on Mr. Moody!"

Does God have a monopoly on your life? If not, why not? Sooner or later, if you continue to knowingly refuse to submit to God or deliberately continue to reserve certain "untouchable" areas in your life from Him, your fellowship with Him can and will be broken. And that's not good!

QUESTIONS:

1. Identify any area(s) of your life in the past where you have found that you failed God, and sincerely ask forgiveness.
2. Reflect upon how wonderful it feels to be forgiven for a past failure, and now turn your attention to the task of taking submission seriously by avoiding rebellion against God.

PRAYER:

O God, we realize from our Lord's Prayer that "Your will being done in earth as it is in heaven" is Your chief desire. *Your* will simply cannot be done if *our* will is being done. The only difference between heaven and hell is that heaven does Your will, and hell fails to. So help us to take submission to Your will very seriously. For Christ's sake, amen.

Lesson 30: "Knockoff Christianity" or
The Essence of True Religion

"Let your kingdom come. Let your will be done on earth as it is done in heaven."

Matthew 6:10 (God's Word)

The need for perfect submission arises because God cannot freely express Himself through anyone who is not perfectly submitted to Him. A musician cannot perfectly express himself with his instrument if it has any will of its own. It must be perfectly compliant and under his control entirely.

Similarly, we, as disciples, must be perfectly compliant and under God's control entirely if He is to express Himself to and through us. All self-interest, self-will, personal ambitions, self-serving religious efforts, and even many religious traditions prevent God from freely expressing Himself through His instruments. Perfect submission gives God the freedom to remake us from the inside out into the beautiful person He intended for us to be. We are then completely open and free to obey whatever His Spirit leads us to do. We can truly *"let His kingdom come."*

The power of God working within us is the essence of true religion. Somehow, in most of our minds, religion is man working as hard as he can *for* God when true religion is really God working as hard as *He* can *in* man! There is a huge difference between the two. Quite simply, human beings *cannot* do the works of God.

Only God Himself can do the works of God. True discipleship is not us trying to *imitate* Christ but moving ourselves out of His way (submission) so that *He* can live His own life through ours. This business of trying to *imitate* Christ results in nothing more than "knockoff Christianity!" And the world is getting fed up and wants to see the *real* thing.

True religion must be God Himself working within us, not merely us trying to be good and godly. He is not *helping* us to be good. It is not a case of Him saving us and cleaning us up then giving us a little push, and we can "take it from here on our own." Within our "flesh dwells no good thing" (Romans 7:18, KJV), so we are going to desperately need a daily act of God Himself from here on out. Our "good" must truly *be* God Himself doing it in us. He wants to express *His* grace, *His* love, *His* power, *His* divine wisdom, *His* "God-ness," *His* very life, through us. *That is true, authentic religion!*

And this can happen only if we radically submit ourselves to Him. *That is our chief task, the one and only thing we are responsible for. Submit so He can work.* If it is *God's* love working in me, then it will never run out. If it is *His* forgiveness, then it can go on forever, no matter what the wound I may have suffered. If it is *God's* peace working in me, then it will be limitless and "pass all understanding" (Philippians 4:7)! That is why to still have peace in some situations simply doesn't make sense! "I give you *My* peace," Jesus promised, "not like the world's peace" (John 14:27), which depends on circumstances being favorable and ideal.

Paul summed this up very well in Philippians 2:13: "[For] it is God who produces in you the desires and actions that please him" (God's Word). That defines true religion: God is doing it all. Otherwise, we ourselves are doing it, and that is not the way it's supposed to work. So every day, our prayer must be, "Lord, live Your life in me." This is what Paul wrote to the Galatians: "I have been crucified with Christ. It is no longer I who live, but Christ who lives in me" (Galatians 2:20).

Albert B. Simpson, founder of The Christian and Missionary Alliance during the holiness revival of the late 1800s, wrote a song, "Abiding and Confiding," which expresses this point:

I have learned the wondrous secret of abiding in the Lord;
I have found the strength and sweetness of confiding in His word.
I have tasted life's pure fountain; I am drinking of His blood;
I have lost myself in Jesus, I am sinking into God.

I am crucified with Jesus, and He lives and dwells in me.
I have ceased from all my struggling, 'Tis no longer I, but He.
All my will is yielded to Him, And His Spirit reigns within,
And His precious blood each moment keeps me cleansed and free from sin.

All my cares I cast upon Him, and He bears them all away;
All my fears and griefs I tell Him, all my needs from day to day.
All my strength I draw from Jesus, By His breath I live and move.
Even His very mind He gives me, and His faith, and life, and love.

For my words, I take His wisdom, for my works His Spirit's power,
For my ways, His gracious presence guards and guides me every hour.
Of my heart, He is the portion, of my joy the ceaseless spring,
Savior, Sanctifier, Keeper, Glorious Lord and loving King!

Chorus: I'm abiding in the Lord, and confiding in His Word,
And I'm hiding, safely hiding in the bosom of His love.

Many times, we Christians sing songs or make statements that voice the concept that we exalt and worship God and give Him the power and glory. But all this rings hollow if we don't really give Him the absolute power over our own lives. In this sin-cursed, Satan-ruled, perversely driven world, God's influence is only as strong as we, His children, permit it to be by giving Him total influence over *us*.

And it's obvious that He doesn't have this total influence over all of us. Otherwise, the world would be a totally different place. *His* "will would be done on earth as it is in heaven!" This explains much of society's problems today: *It is increasingly difficult to find true disciples of Christ who will give God the power to rule over their lives in every way.* If God truly had His way, if He were really expressing Himself through everyone who claims to be a Christian, if every life were really *Jesus Christ* living in that religious person, then the Church and the world would be radically different!

Then the world would see *true* religion. There would be absolutely no selfish Christians, totally wrapped up in their own lives; no idle, unused Christians, sitting on the shelf like an unused tool while the world precipitously falls into hell; no Christians who could just apathetically watch their neighbors be lost forever; and no church folks who could spend most of their time fighting with other church folks in endless, ubiquitous church intrigues. Churches where nobody gets saved or healed this year would cease to exist! There would be fewer homeless, unloved, lonely, spiritually dying people, and society would be revolutionized—if Jesus were truly living *His* life in all of us.

> Listen to this profound truth: *True and pure Christianity is God downloading heaven to earth! That is not happening very often or in very many places. This explains why the world,*

especially Western society, is getting sick of and cynical about Christianity. In today's world, when people "have a problem with religion," it is simply because they are not seeing heaven downloaded to Earth!

Let's take this personal: Is it happening with *you?* That is, when did *you* get your last download? Yesterday? Last week? Last year? Can't say when? Maybe *never?* So perhaps *you* are what's wrong with this world! Perhaps *you* are what's wrong with Christianity! When Jesus looks out over the world, make sure that He will find at least *one* life *totally* open and surrendered to Him—*yours!*

QUESTIONS:

1. Identify any area(s) of your life where you are doing the religious works you do just because you feel like they are a mandated duty and you are afraid *not* to do them, not because you love God or because He's moving within you to do them.
2. How can the Christian church as a whole experience the moving of God's Spirit on His people so that He is living, breathing, loving, and momentarily motivating it?
3. What can *your* church do to bring this to pass?

PRAYER:

Lord Jesus, I realize this is the main problem with the Church, the world, and my own life: *There simply are not enough people allowing You to live Your life in and through them.* Lord God, from this time forward, I ask You to enable me to move myself out of the way and "let Your kingdom come, and Your will be done in earth—this 'earth' I call myself!" For Christ's sake, amen.

CHAPTER FIVE
RADICAL SUBMISSION IN THE HOME

Lesson 31: Radical Submission and Raising Children

"Submit yourselves to one another because of your reverence for Christ."

Ephesians 5:21 (GNB)

In addition to the many ways in which radical submission will revolutionize a Christian's personal life, it will also revolutionize his or her home life. *The degree of peace and success in the home depends directly on the degree of submissiveness of the family members to God's will and God's way.*

The children must be submissive to the parents, which is being submissive to God: "Children obey your parents in all things for this is well-pleasing unto the Lord" (Colossians 3:20, KJV). The wife must be submissive to the husband, which is being submissive to God: "Wives submit yourselves unto your own husbands, as unto the Lord" (Ephesians 5:22, KJV). And husbands must be submissively loving to their wives, which is being submissive to God: "Husbands, love your wives, even as Christ loved the church and gave Himself for it" (Ephesians 5:25, KJV). Thus, the wife is submissive to the husband's lead; he is submissive to her need. And all of this is being submissive to God: "Submitting yourselves one to another in the fear of God" (Ephesians 5:21, KJV).

Submissiveness is best learned when a person is young. "It is good for a man that he bear the yoke [of divine disciplinary dealings] in his youth" (Lamentations 3:27, AMP). Therefore, we'll first speak to parents concerning the instilling of submissiveness in their children.

We live in a damnably permissive society. It is damnable because a person who cannot submit to God, parents, authority, moral standards, social structures and institutions, etc., will not be able to control his or her selfishness and is therefore doomed to trouble on earth and hell in the afterlife. *The best thing parents can do for their children is to train them to be able to submit—to parents, to social authorities, to moral standards, and to God.* Failure means that that child will have a difficult time in this life and the next.

Susanna Wesley, mother of nineteen children including John and Charles, said this:

> When the will of a child is totally subdued, and it is brought to revere and stand in awe of the parents, then a great many childish follies and inadvertencies [accidents] may be passed by. Some should be overlooked and taken no notice of, and others mildly reproved; but no willful transgression ought ever to be forgiven children without chastisement less or more, as the nature and circumstances of the case may require. I insist on conquering of the will of children betimes [early] because this is the only strong and rational foundation of a religious education, without which both precept and example will be ineffectual. But when this is thoroughly done, then a child is capable of being governed by the reason and piety of its parents, till its

own understanding comes to maturity, and the principles of religion have taken root in the mind.

I cannot yet dismiss the subject. As self-will is the root of all sin and misery, so whatever cherishes this in children ensures their after wretchedness and irreligion; whatever checks and mortifies [self-will] promotes their future happiness and piety. This is still more evident if we further consider *that religion is nothing else than doing the will of God and not our own;* that the one grand impediment to our temporal and eternal happiness being this self-will, no indulgence of it can be trivial, no denial unprofitable. Heaven or hell depends on this alone so that the parent who studies to subdue [self-will] in his child works together with God in renewing and saving a soul. The parent who indulges it does the Devil's work; makes religion impracticable, salvation unattainable, and does all that in him lies to *damn his child body and soul forever.*[9]

When a Christian becomes a parent, he or she must consent to be a parent *living under submission to God.* The parents then must dedicate the child back to God and become merely the *managers* of God's child. As such, the parents accept the responsibility for *everything* in that child's life. They cannot opt out or neglect the child. They must not fail or throw in the towel. They cannot delegate this responsibility to other people because it is theirs alone. They cannot afford to be inconsistent because they are tired, lazy, upset, or unwilling to be inconvenienced.

They cannot "chicken out" because being a parent is difficult and often unpopular. They are not in it just to be the boss or to satisfy their need to be needed, but to build character and self-discipline within their children *before* they reach the age of unconquerable self-willfulness that will inevitably lead them astray from God, into destructive habits, character, and lifestyles.

QUESTIONS:

1. The concept of practicing submissiveness in the home is almost anathema today. Preach it too strong, and you might split your church (e.g., Southern Baptists in 1998!). Why do you think it is frowned on today?
2. How do you think parents today would feel about "conquering the will of the child"?
3. What is your interpretation/application of Ephesians 5:21–33?
4. Do you agree with Susanna Wesley's summary of religion: "*Religion is nothing else than doing the will of God and not our own*"?

PRAYER:

O Heavenly Father, help us to practice the Spirit of Christ, Who is "Submission Personified," in our homes and relationships. Help us to raise obedient and respectful children. Help every Christian wife to practice submitting to her husband's lead. Help every Christian husband to practice loving his wife as You "loved the Church and gave yourself for it," which is nothing more than submitting to, considering, and allowing himself to be governed by his wife's needs. And help all of us to lovingly submit to each other and to You. Let this be the spirit that rules our families, our lives, and our churches. In Jesus' name, amen.

Lesson 32: More About Children, Submission, and Discipline

"Respect your father and mother, and you will live a long and
successful life in the land I am giving you."

Deuteronomy 5:16 (CEV)

The purpose of having a child learn submission is so that he can learn how to be a disciplined person early in life. Our society is filled with millions of very undisciplined people, not able to control themselves very well. They are generally ruled by their selfish desires, emotions, whims, and wishes. Their biggest concerns are comfort, convenience, and having things go their way. We've been called an "addictive society," with nearly everybody living under the control of something.

Submission to authority first requires an external discipline, with the goal of it becoming internal self-discipline by the time the child reaches adulthood. If submission is not taught, then self-discipline is never achieved.

My years of teaching mathematics are a prime example. Most of the kids were very undisciplined, finding it difficult to concentrate for a long period of class time or to do assignments at home. Some could barely sit still, keep their mouths shut, or stay off their phones. Dozens were taking behavior-modifying medicines but were still easily distracted. Their parents were barely any better, siding with their kids' whenever a problem at school arose and excusing their kids' errant behavior, failure to do homework, or refusal to meet whatever the standards were. So, we played lots of math games. But they don't call mathematics one of the "disciplines" for nothing: Sooner or later, a person has got to buckle down and do some heavy-duty thinking. And an undisciplined person with an undisciplined mind simply cannot do this. This is why, in general, our American children are not very good at meeting any kind of rigorous academic standards, especially in math, science, and technology. And every few years, our educational system revises and "dumbs down" the academic standards, the standardized tests, the college entrance exams, and other measuring sticks of learning because too many kids simply can't pass.

Submission to God just about *requires* a parent to spank a child when necessary. God's Word teaches that it is the *only* way to produce submissiveness in the child (Proverbs 13:24; 19:18; 22:15; 23:13, 14; 29:15, 17; Hebrews 12:6–11). Indeed, Proverbs 23:13–14 in *The Message* states it very succinctly: "Don't be afraid to correct your young ones; a spanking won't kill them. A good spanking, in fact, might save them from something worse than death." The fact is, like animals, human beings—adults and children, but especially children—are most efficiently trained through the judicious use of a combination of negative and positive rewards, including physical pain and pleasure. Most humans learn life lessons best when we learn them the "hard way," i.e. when it involves painful experiences. *Children cannot truly learn submission without some type of physical pain being inflicted.*

Other methods of behavior modification can help, but they all involve some form of negotiation, bribery, complex reasoning, or punishments that obtain a lesser degree of obedience while allowing the child to retain his self-will—and remain *undisciplined.* True discipline requires a higher level of submission to authority, to rules, and to self-denial. Consequence-based training doesn't usually work very well on very young children because their reasoning ability is not yet fully developed, they are more under the control of their fickle emotions, and it is often quite difficult to find meaningful consequences, rewards, and choices that are really able to manipulate their behavior. What does a "time out" really mean to a one-year-old? Send them to their rooms for punishment, and they merely go to sleep. Plus, they forget almost immediately *why* they were sent to their rooms. Still, it is not too early to train a one-year-old how to obey and submit to the parents' will. If a child is old enough to show self-willfulness, then they are old enough to be *trained* that such behavior is not allowed. "Train [not merely educate] a child in the way he should go, and even when he is old he will not turn away from it" (Proverbs 22:6, GW).

So, the immediate, deliberate (but not anger-motivated), and strategically targeted infliction of a small degree of pain will effectively *train* a child and bring him under submission to the will of his parents. Some children appear to be naturally "easy-going," especially during the early childhood years, so their parents often decide to skip physical correction altogether. But many times, these "easy-going" children become very willful, less cooperative, and difficult during the teen years, simply because their wills have never become submissive to the parents'.

Submission to God requires a parent to get the courage to say no and set limits for the child and to *always and consistently* do what is best for a child no matter how much the child protests or how reluctant the parent himself might feel. Thus, a parent cannot afford to go along with the child's whims, fancies, and temperament but to bring those childish whims, fancies, and temperaments under submission. The parent does not cater to the *child's* program, schedule, desires, etc. Instead, the parent labors to train the child by bringing the child under the *parent's* program, schedule, desires, structure, etc. Far too many parents today have fallen under the control of their children instead of the opposite being true.

Likewise, far too many children, Christian and otherwise, are being stuck with labels that tell the world they should not even be *expected* to control their behavior: ADD, ADHD, learning disabled, "can't pay attention," unmotivated, lazy, "need more time to find themselves," etc. And psychologists are continually coining new labels: ODD (Oppositional Defiant Disorder), ARD (Adolescent Rebellion Disorder), and CD (Conduct Disorder) are three of the newest, which are really euphemisms for a spoiled, untrained child. I recently asked a child psychiatrist, "what do you professionals call a 'spoiled brat' today?" and he handed me a lengthy brochure on Oppositional Defiant Disorder (ODD). Whatever the "disorder," we explain it away by saying, "He is just a *bad* child. I remember his old grandfather was like that. This is the family curse…" But really, there are no "bad" children, just *untrained* children. And *all* kids can be trained.

Now it is true that much of our personality is inherited. Our genes do determine a lot of our human tendencies. But that is not the end of the story. Environment and nurture, i.e., upbringing, plays an important role. After we are born with these tendencies, we are allowed—by our indulgent parents and our permissive society—to grow up without much consistent training and loving discipline, usually getting our own way, never regularly being forced to do what we hate to do but *ought* to do, never having to concentrate on anything for any length of time, never being trained to endure hardness, never being forced to work, never having to fit ourselves into a structure or program that builds character, always shielded from suffering the negative consequences of our bad decisions, etc. From day one, we are allowed by everything and everyone around us to grow up basically as undisciplined brats.

Then, at eighteen years old, everybody wants to blame Grandpa's genes for why Junior can't keep a job, finish school, maintain a serious, productive family relationship, demonstrate fiscal responsibility, or the like. Listen, it's not Grandpa's fault, and it's not a *generational* curse. It's a curse, all right, but the family allowed it to be created in *this* generation, not a previous one! It is merely the awful result of living life in *rebellion* to God rather than in submission to His principles of sober and sensible living. Parents live selfishly, lazily, and ignorantly and then wonder why their children cannot fit into anything productive.

QUESTIONS:

1. Do you agree with the idea that parents have the duty to force the child into the parent's program? That is, do you believe a child should submit to his/her parents?

PRAYER:

Father God, please give parents the courage and wisdom to know how to direct their children into the way they *should* go. In His Name, amen.

Lesson 33: Submission to God Saves Marriages

"Submit yourselves to one another because of your reverence for Christ"
("the fear of God" in the KJV)

Ephesians 5:21 (GNB)

Marriages fail because of a lack of submission to God, which can also be called "reverence for Christ" or the "fear of God." Contrary to popular belief, the Bible teaches that marriage is permanent, according to the God who invented it. People, including most Christians, refuse to accept and practice this. Problems arise, troubles occur, pressures increase, and before long, couples claim to have irreconcilable differences and incompatibility. They "grow apart;" they "fall out of love" with each other, and sometimes "fall in love" with someone else (as if they just can't help themselves!). So, they feel justified to throw in the towel on their marriages, to "cut their losses and start over" with someone else, this time a real "soul mate."

The problem is this is all completely contrary to the principle of submission to God. God intended marriage to be permanent. So, every couple must fight desperately for their marriage to succeed. There is no easy way out because of inconvenience, personal discomfort, or so-called "falling out of love" (Matthew 19:3–9). This is how submission to God would keep a marriage from falling apart: When your spouse causes you some kind of disappointment or pain, even *great* pain, submission to God requires you to forgive and reconcile. If you refuse to forgive, then it is obvious that you are in rebellion, not submission, to God. When either partner—the offending one or the offended one—chooses to live selfishly and considers only themselves, they are not living in submission to God. Living selfishly is the number one destroyer of marriages.

Listen carefully, because this statement is always true: *If the marriage falls apart, it is not only because of what your spouse did but because one or both of you are in rebellion against God! Two true disciples of Christ can live together—happily—for a lifetime over any and all difficulties.* It is simply scandalous, as the kids say, for all the divorces among Christian marriages to occur, even among big-time, influential ministers.

Thus, you must not focus on what your spouse did. It could have been very wrong and unfair, perhaps outrageous. But if you plan to stay in fellowship with God and keep your relationship with *Him* on friendly terms, then you *must* forgive your spouse. Your focus is on God and maintaining your peace with Him. You forgive your spouse, not because they are so apologetic (because they might not be), nor because what they did or said was inconsequential (because it might have been very significant), nor because you want to please your spouse (because you might not really like them at the moment), *but because you want to please God and you "fear" and "reverence" Him.*

It's between you and *God,* not just between you and your *spouse.* Thus, though your spouse sometimes does not even deserve it, they reap the benefit of your willingness to submit your anger, personal needs and desires, and feelings of injury to God. A marriage where both partners are submitting to God like this is a marriage that will *never* fall apart.

IMPORTANT DISCLAIMER: It should be noted that nothing written in this book should be taken as an excuse for abuse. That is, when we talk about submission, even if we quote Ephesians 5:22 (*"Wives submit yourselves to your own husbands"*), this is not to instruct them to accept abuse of any type from their husbands (or vice-versa). If the wife, husband, or children are being abused, we do not believe the Bible requires them to remain in that situation and meekly accept the abuse in the name of being "submissive." That is not *biblical* submission. In biblical submission, submission is submitting to *God*, not to some kind of abuse—physical, sexual, verbal, mental, or spiritual abuse. Instead, we believe and teach that in such abusive situations, the Bible permits the abused party and the children, if necessary, to remove themselves to some safe place, seek help, and not put themselves at risk of abuse anymore.

QUESTIONS:

1. Just how true is the assertion, "Marriages fail because of a lack of submission to God"? How does it fit with this statement: "Living selfishly is the number one destroyer of marriages"?
2. How has the church misused the instruction in Ephesians 5:22: *"Wives submit yourselves to your own husbands"*?

PRAYER:

Merciful Lord, with humble hearts, we acknowledge that many times we want to put the blame on one party in a marriage but help us to admit that both parties should practice submitting to God for the peace and continuance of the marriage. Help us to see that each party having the determination to please God is the best foundation for their relationship. In the name of our Savior, amen.

Lesson 34: Submission to God Can Restore Love

"They replied, 'Moses allowed a man to write a bill of divorce and to put her away.' [Deut. 24:1–4.]. But Jesus said to them, 'Because of your hardness of heart [your condition of insensibility to the call of God] he wrote you this precept in your Law'"

Mark 10:4–5 (AMP)

Here is another example of how submission to God saves marriages. Many people often state, "I have fallen out of love with my husband (or wife). He or she has done so much awful stuff; I just don't have feelings for him/her anymore and never will again." Then they proceed to either live in that depressed condition for the rest of their lives or, most likely, divorce him/her and find somebody else they can "really love."

The fact is, God does not give a person a "get-out-of-the-marriage" free card just for falling out of love, simply because He has made a way possible for that person to fall back into love. That way is submission to God. If a wife or husband will submit themselves to God's principle of truth that marriage is permanent, if s/he will submit their damaged and dead feelings to God for Him to revive them, if s/he can be *willing* for God to give them love for their spouse again—then God can restore it. He will direct their steps until full love for their spouse has been restored.

The problem many spouses have is that they are not willing—that is, not submitted—for God to give them love again for a husband or wife whose past behavior has so destroyed their love. An offended wife often feels too proud to even *want* her love for her husband to be restored; it might make her look humiliated before others. An offended husband often feels the same way. So, s/he goes on saying, "I have fallen out of love with you, and I don't think I can ever love you again."

Christians should remember that marriage is a covenant, like God practices it, not merely a contract, as the world practices it. A contract is an *agreement* between two parties that describes what each party promises to do to benefit the other. If one party violates the contract by failing to keep up his end of the contract, then the other is free to cancel the contract, making it null and void. On the other hand, a *covenant* is a *permanent relationship* in which both parties promise to hold up their ends *regardless* of whether the other party keeps their part of the agreement. A violation of a covenant agreement does not break the relationship. A violation by one party doesn't matter as far as the other party's responsibility to continue to do what they agreed to do. A covenant is patterned after God's covenant with His people, Israel, and Christ's covenant with His Bride, the Church. God never gave up on His covenant people Israel, and Jesus will never disown His Church, although both Israel and the Church have had times of unfaithfulness and shameful behavior. Christian marriage is such a covenant.

One famous pastor, Tullian Tchividjian, Billy Graham's grandson, in 2015 filed for divorce from his wife of twenty-one years (with three children) because their marriage was, in the words of their counselor, Paul Tripp, "irreparably broken." Both spouses had cheated, supposedly the wife first, then the husband. "Sadly," the counselor reported, "there are times when the trust is so deeply broken and patterns so set in place that it seems best to recognize that brokenness, cry out for God's grace, mourn, commit to forgiveness, rest in the truths of the Gospel and with a grieved heart move on." In other words, are we to assume that their marriage was beyond *God's* ability to fix and restore it? *God Himself* found it impossible? Of course not! Jesus truly can fix anything, even a horrifically broken marriage between two horrifically broken people.

So, when a marriage seemingly cannot be fixed and is "irreparably broken," that simply means that one or both parties *are not willing* for it to be fixed. Somebody has refused to radically submit to God. *Somebody is holding on to their selfishness and justifying their sin.* Restoring trust requires a person to first trust in God. Why? Because trust always involves a large degree of risk and uncertainty, which most people simply are not willing to subject themselves to, especially after they have been so badly hurt by their spouses. But in order to please God, allow Him to rebuild trust and love, and restore the marriage, each spouse simply *must* be willing to make themselves vulnerable again until reconciliation is achieved. Self-protection simply is not radical submission to God, no matter how justifiable it might seem to be.[a]

In 2013, another famous pastor, Ron Carpenter, Jr., of the Redemption World Outreach Center of Greenville, SC, whose wife of twenty-three years had cheated on him for many years, refused to even consider reconciliation until God spoke to him through Jesus' words in Mark 10:5 (KJV): "*Moses let you divorce your wives,*" but it was only "*because of the hardness of your hearts,*" i.e., "*your condition of insensibility to the call of God*" (AMP). He said that God told him to call his wife at the rehab facility she had checked herself into and promise her that he would not abandon her. Out

a. See http://www.christianpost.com/news/paul-tripp-says-billy-grahams-grandson-tullian-tchividjians-divorce-is-necessary-because-marriage-is-irreparably-broken-143982/.

of what he said was a "sheer fear of God" and not "lovey-dovey feelings," he did what he felt God wanted him to do. And their marriage was successfully restored.[b] Together, they now sponsor, among other ministries, "Marriage Rendezvous" conferences.[c]

But take another look at Jesus' true attitude against divorce in Matthew 19:8–9 (NIV): "Jesus replied, 'Moses permitted you to divorce your wives because your hearts were hard. But it was not this way from the beginning. I tell you that anyone who divorces his wife, except for sexual immorality, and marries another woman commits adultery.'" Or, from The Message: "Jesus said, 'Moses provided for divorce as a concession to your hardheartedness, but it is not part of God's original plan. I'm holding you to the original plan and holding you liable for adultery if you divorce your faithful wife and then marry someone else. I make an exception in cases where the spouse has committed adultery.'"

Most Christians miss one of the main messages in this passage. They faithfully quote the "Exception Clause," which gives them the right to divorce because of sexual immorality. *But they fail to see that the whole reason divorce was given in the first place was because of their hard, rebellious hearts!* They fail to realize that just because they biblically *can* divorce doesn't mean that they *must* or *should* divorce. *Obviously, Jesus expects them to do everything possible to reconcile and restore the marriage, which is God's "original plan." Divorce is not His "original plan"* and has always been the absolute last *resort*.

How could it be otherwise? Wouldn't the God who plainly states, "I hate divorce" (Malachi 2:16, NLT), desire most of all that troubled spouses reconcile and keep their marriages intact? Knowing that divorce steals, kills, deeply wounds, and destroys

---

b. See http://www.charismanews.com/us/42301-ron-carpenter-en-lists-td-jakes-to-oversee-miracle-marriage-reconciliation.

c. See http://www.roncarpenter.com/marriageconf/.

souls (and bodies and minds, as well) that God deeply loves and gave Himself to heal and restore, wouldn't His biggest desire be to fix the people and the problems and avoid divorce at any cost, no matter what the problem? He is a God of love, forgiveness, second chances, reconciliation, and restoration. Wouldn't He expect the couple to do everything within their power to fix the individuals and fix the marriage before dissolving their marriage covenant, which is symbolic of and patterned after His own love covenant with His Bride, the Church? *So even though He provides an exception to get out of a marriage, His true desire is that the couple fixes themselves, whatever the problem, and save the marriage.* Too much is eternally at stake.

If, in the Spirit of Christ (humility, forgiveness, love, and willingness to do God's will), each partner practices radical submission to God, they *will* reconcile and restore the marriage. But if in a spirit and attitude contrary to the Spirit of Christ, they harden against each other and cannot reconcile, then they should each realize that *the indictment is against them:* their own *"hardness of heart"* is what prevents it. *The cause of the divorce is no longer what one or both partners may have done but their unwillingness to be reconciled.* Their own *"insensibility to the call of God"* (AMP), in which they cannot or refuse to hear the Holy Spirit and the heart of God, makes reconciliation and restoration impossible. And no true Christian would be comfortable facing God with hardness of heart, a condition that Jesus condemns according to this passage in Matthew 19. Actually, they should "Examine [them]selves to see whether [they] are still in [and true to] the Christian faith" (2 Corinthians 13:5, God's Word) because it now involves their own relationship with God Himself.

This is exactly the meaning and appropriate application of Ephesians 5:21: "Submit yourselves to one another because of your reverence for Christ" ('fear of God' in the KJV). The next verse requires wives to submit themselves to and reverence their husbands, "*as unto the Lord.*" And in verse 25, husbands are required to love their wives "*even as,*" i.e., to the same degree, "*as Christ loved the Church...*" The reason a married individual treats his/her spouse with love or reverence under all circumstances is because that individual loves God, fears God, and wants to please God and measure up to *His* standard—*independently* of the spouse's actions. *The fear of God and the desire not to displease Him keeps a Christian in the marriage.*

True *agape* love for one's spouse means that an individual cannot give up on their spouse any sooner than God gives up on us for our own repeated failures. Perhaps a temporary separation might be feasible for safety (as in abuse) or co-dependency (as in addiction), but the goal should always be to fix the problem or the person, then counsel and work together for reconciliation.

This is especially true if children are involved because divorce affects them traumatically and permanently. "The kids will adjust," selfish adults always say, and, true, the kids *do* adjust, but almost always in a *negative* way. Evidence shows that parental divorce causes major problems for children that last into and throughout adulthood:

- Fifty percent of children of divorce move into poverty after the divorce.[d]

- Teens from divorced households are three times more likely to need psychological help.[e]

---

d. http://www.heritage.org/marriage-and-family/report/the-effects-divorce-america

e. https://townhall.com/columnists/laurahollis/2015/09/10/an-epidemic-of-denial-n2050403

- Study after study has shown that children from divorced families suffer more physical ailments and perform at a lower level academically.[f]

- Children of divorced parents are roughly two times more likely to drop out than children from intact families.[g]

- A study of children six years after a parental marriage breakup revealed that even after all that time to make the "adjustments" their parents expected them to make, these children still tended to be "lonely, unhappy, anxious and insecure. *(Wallerstein, "The Long-Term Effects of Divorce on Children."*[h]

- People who come from broken homes are twice as likely to attempt suicide than those who do not come from broken homes.[i]

- Children of divorce have relationship problems: they have a 26 percent lower rate of getting married in the first place.[j]

- After they do get married, the risk of divorce is 50 percent higher when one spouse comes from a divorced home and 200 percent higher risk when both of them do.[k]

---

f. https://www.owenbylaw.com/blog/2018/october/statistics-children-divorce/

g. McLanahan, Sandefur, Growing Up With a Single Parent: What Hurts, What Helps, Harvard University Press 1994; http://www.marriage-success-secrets.com/statistics-about-children-and-divorce.html.

h. Journal of the American Academy of Child and Adolescent Psychiatry 1991; https://www.jaacap.org/article/S0890-8567(09)64550-0/pdf.

i. https://www.thespruce.com/children-of-divorce-in-america-statistics-1270390

j. http://www.divorcereform.org/mel/rhistories.html

k. Nicholas Wolfinger, professor of family and consumer studies at the University of Utah and author of *Understanding the Divorce Cycle: The*

Of course, some people think that some of these stats are old and outdated, and the increasingly common practice of joint custody of the children has changed the negative consequences associated with divorce. However, here's another very alarming, relatively recent stat about our young people (19–25 years old) in America: *One-half (50 percent) of them have a diagnosable mental health disorder* [e.g., personality disorders (obsessive, anti-social and paranoid behaviors), depression, anxiety, suicidal ideation, eating disorders, self-injury, and substance/drug abuse, etc.], almost all of it being traced back to their broken, ill-formed, dysfunctional, and collapsing families.[1]

And while you are looking at that, also check out these more recent facts from world-renown psychiatrist, Dr. Luis Rojas Marcos, in *A Silent Tragedy in Our Homes*: "A 37 percent increase in adolescent depression has been noted, and there has been a 200 percent increase in the suicide rate in children aged ten to fourteen in the last fifteen years."[m]

Knowing these facts, it is truly unbelievable that so many Christians still dissolve their marriages at such a tragically alarming rate. There is no way in the world God is pleased with this, but apparently, they don't seem to care. Pleasing themselves is more important than pleasing God.

Children of Divorce in Their Own Marriages, quoted at http://www.cnn.com/2010/LIVING/09/22/divorced.parents.children.marriage/index.html.
l. See the reports at http://usatoday30.usatoday.com/news/health/2008-12-02-mentalhealth_N.htm and https://townhall.com/columnists/laurahollis/2015/09/10/an-epidemic-of-denial-n2050403.
m. http://www.racinelutheran.org/wp-content/uploads/2019/12/PaP-A-Silent-Tragedy-article-PDF.pdf

HELP By Erica Campbell of "Mary, Mary" (with Lecrae)
http://www.youtube.com/watch?v=J1e6zqqySHw

"...Said 'I do,' but to tell the truth, Sometimes I don't.
But it ain't about my will. It's all about what *You* want..."

I have always openly admitted that my wife loves me today, not because I have been such a perfect husband who never caused her any pain or made her cry, but because she loves *God* more than she loves *me*. He talks to her and enables her to come back and keep loving me, despite me being me. I consider myself to be a very good husband, but even the best husband can be an awful trial sometimes! If my wife did not love and fear God so greatly and want to please Him so badly, she would have walked out on me (or killed me) a long time ago!

So then, it is her submission to God and her love for God, not my perfect goodness, which has kept us together, through the rough times and normal storms of life, for more than forty years. It's something between God and her; sometimes, I seem to be somewhat incidental! On occasion, she has even plainly said it: "I'm really not forgiving you because I feel like it, but because I love God and I want to stay in fellowship with Him." Only God knows how much I really appreciate *Him* for doing *me* this favor! And she would say the same thing about me.

Now all this works for this simple reason: *Marriages fail because somebody in the marriage is being selfish.* It may be one or both parties. One partner might be reacting selfishly to the selfish actions of the other. But radical submission to God removes selfishness from the entire life of a Christian, including his or her marriage. Radical submission causes a wife to reverence her husband no matter what and a husband to love his wife unconditionally. *Thus, when neither party insists on living selfishly, their marriage becomes indestructible.* They can truly stay together "as long as they both shall live."

Because divorce among Christians is always an indication that selfishness in one or both partners prevailed, anyone considering marriage to a divorced Christian should be extremely careful. *How does one determine that the selfishness that wrecked the first marriage is not found in the divorced person you want to marry, especially knowing that a divorce is* never *the fault of only one partner?* How do you know that the person you want to marry does not have a hard, spiritually insensitive heart and fails to listen to the desires of God? How would you know that they have truly identified why their first marriage failed, what fault was their own, and how they will prevent it from happening all over again? Do they have a forgiving heart? Are they still carrying the "baggage" that affected their first marriage? Have they been healed of old wounds and made "whole" yet? Have they learned any lessons, are they repentant, or are they just switching partners without any major changes or inner healing happening within themselves? Are they submissive to God? It pays to be very careful in these situations!

QUESTIONS:

1. List several reasons that Christians use to justify ending their marriages and discuss how radical submission would help them overcome.
2. What do you think is God's attitude about the high rate of divorce among Christians?

PRAYER:

Almighty God, Redeemer, Restorer, Eternal Salvager, God of mercy, and also, Creator of Marriage, the first and the ultimate human relationship: It is with humble hearts that we bow and acknowledge that, in spite of Your sacrifice to heal our relationships, so many times we persist in destroying them. Forgive us for our failures in the area of marriage. Especially forgive the Christian Church for failing to hold a higher, more rigorous standard for our people regarding marriage, allowing them to be selfish, hardhearted, insensitive, and contrary so often to Your original desires. Forgive us for our individual failures. Let there be a mighty spiritual renewal among us concerning marriage for the benefit of families, society, and Your Kingdom as a whole. In Jesus' name, amen.

Lesson 35: Holiness—God's Ultimate Purpose of Marriage

"That's why we can be so sure that every detail in our lives of love for God is worked into something good. God knew what he was doing from the very beginning. He decided from the outset to shape the lives of those who love him along the same lines as the life of his Son. The Son stands first in the line of humanity he restored. We see the original and intended shape of our lives there in him."

Romans 8:28–29 (The Message)

It would be truly wonderful if every Christian couple could realize that God's primary purpose in their marriage is not to make them happy but holy. Romans 8:28–30 tells us plainly that God's ultimate purpose is to produce beings who are "conformed to the image of His Son," Jesus Christ, so that Christ is merely "the firstborn among many brethren." So, since God's chief desire is to produce Christlikeness in as many people as possible, He uses every situation in our lives to achieve this goal. This definitely includes marriage.

Even though two people claim to be "soul mates" and believe themselves to be highly compatible, they will soon find that they have many differences, after all, sometimes major differences. They simply do not think exactly alike or have the exact same desires. Besides that, people bring all kinds of baggage to a marriage, much of which may be unseen and unknown until it starts popping up during the close interactions of marriage.

This inevitably causes friction of some degree and presents issues that must be worked out. This working out process requires both spouses to deny themselves, swallow their pride, give in to the other, delay their own gratification, forgive and ask forgiveness repeatedly, overlook the other's weaknesses constantly, defer to each other over and over, etc. It won't take long for each of them to realize their own pre-existent character flaws, selfishness, emotional wounds, insecurities, fears, and other personal weaknesses.

The interactions of marriage faithfully and inevitably reveal all of this. Then it is up to us to allow those revelations to point out to us the areas where we need spiritual grace and strength. For example, the *real* reason why you got mad is not *what* your wife said or *how* she said it but because you yourself had an internal weakness that couldn't handle what she said. Work on your weaknesses, and it won't matter what she says. She wouldn't be able to make Jesus Christ mad!

So, the *real* problem is in *you,* not *her.* She didn't cause your problem; your own flaws did! God is working on you in the trenches of your marriage. You must thank God for permitting you to see your weaknesses, submit to His sanctifying, cleansing, and refining process, and cry out to Him to heal and remake you in those areas. By doing this, your marriage has the awesome potential to make you spiritually and emotionally stronger and more Christ-like. Through your marriage, God is making you *holy.*

Notice this process described in a Christian rap song "Boasting" by Lecrae:

BOASTING By Lecrae (ft. Anthony Evans)
https://www.youtube.com/watch?v=4Ec7ofMOqVM

"...Patiently you turned my heart away from selfishness.
I volunteer for your sanctifying surgery.
I know the Spirit's purging me of everything that's hurting me.
Remove the veil from my darkened eyes.
So now every morning I open your Word and see the Son rise.
I hope in nothin, boast in nothin, only in your suffering.
I live to show your glory, dying to tell your story."[10]

One young husband once plopped down on our couch and sighed, "I had *no* idea I was so insecure!" Prior to this time, he had been quite confident and sure of himself, bordering on arrogance, but his new wife obviously was helping him discover his weaknesses and shortcomings. Living with another person is the quickest way for God to uncover your own un-Christlikeness—and transform *you*. Pastor Rick Warren sums up this concept in this concise quote: "Marriage is God's primary tool for teaching us unselfishness, sensitivity, sacrifice, and mature love."[n] The process might hurt, but amen to that truth!

---

n. https://sermons.faithlife.com/sermons/89848-six-characteristics-of-a-satisfying-marriage

QUESTIONS:

1. The awareness that God uses marriage to help make His people holy and spiritually mature is very important. What effect would this knowledge and awareness have on the high rate of divorce among Christians?

2. How *thankful* are you when God permits another person to do or say things that help reveal your faults and weaknesses so you can get stronger in those areas? Or do you basically blame that person for doing or saying the "wrong" thing?

PRAYER:

Our Father, we thank You for the way You use the circumstances and situations of normal life, including our marriages, to sanctify, purify, and make holy Your people. Help us to learn how to work along *with* You, not *against* You. Help us to realize that Your chief desire is for us to "*be holy, because [You] are holy.*" Help us to quit fighting You and each other and to learn Radical Submission in our marriages. This holiness will bring us happiness. In Your Son's name, amen.

Lesson 36: Submission Allows God to Move into Your Marriage

"Love is very patient and kind, never jealous or envious, never boastful or proud, never haughty or selfish or rude. Love does not demand its own way. It is not irritable or touchy. It does not hold grudges and will hardly even notice when others do it wrong. It is never glad about injustice, but rejoices whenever truth wins out. If you love someone, you will be loyal to him no matter what the cost. You will always believe in him, always expect the best of him, and always stand your ground in defending him. All the special gifts and powers from God will someday come to an end, but love goes on forever..."

1 Corinthians 13:4–8 (TLB)

I once had a personal experience during our second year of marriage where I despaired so much because of my inability to keep from hurting my wife constantly that I found myself stretched out on the floor desperately crying out to God for spiritual and emotional help. Soon I appeared to be in a trance. "Jesus," I cried, "my wife would be far better off if I could just die now and let her have some peace! She's better off without me! Why don't You just take my life!" Then I saw the Lord reach out His hand to me, saying, "Here's *My* life. Why don't you take *Mine?*"

And in a flash of enlightenment, I realized that *that* was the definition of sanctification and true religion: *Exchanging our own lives for the Lord's*! Immediately I jumped up from the floor, energized forever by that divine revelation. *His* life is beautiful;

mine is quite ugly. *His* life brings peace; mine brings only fear, insecurity, and anxiety. *His* life heals and builds up other people; mine only hurts, wounds, and destroys other people. Yes, let me take *His* life! Let us *all* take His life! Let us submit ourselves and move over and let Christ live *His* life in us!

Marriage quickly reveals another truth: *Every person has a void within that only God can fill and satisfy, and He never intended for another human being, not even a beloved spouse, to be able to fill it.* In other words, only God, not even a "perfect" husband or wife, can fill certain needs within the human heart. Only God, not a romance, can truly heal a heart. Only God, not *any* human relationship, can make a person truly whole and secure.

However, the human tendency is to expect your husband or wife to give you such love that it makes you fully secure or brings you complete satisfaction. Such is our fondest desire. Then we become extremely disappointed when we discover that our spouse fails to completely fill that void. But at their best, they are only human, and, contrary to what most of us thought, it was never intended for them to be able to fill that void in the first place. We must always recognize this fact whenever we feel dissatisfied with our spouse because "our needs are not being met." Keep in mind that, considering the circumstances, personalities, relationship skills, and current level of knowledge, experience, and spiritual development, they might not be capable of meeting those needs at this time. But quitting or finding someone else (who may be even *more* inadequate!) is out of the question.

Thus, it is critical for God's love to kick in at this point when you run out of your own internal emotional resources. Radical submission allows for God's *agape* love to take over in a marriage. Remember that submission to God removes one's selfish desires from the equation, thus permitting God's life and attributes to be expressed and manifested. *This is especially necessary in marriage.* When you submit your disappointment, hurt feelings, and anger to God and let Him have it, He will give you another gear, a turbo, to operate with. Without God's *agape* love taking over, people get tired of forgiving one another, being patient with each other, giving in to each other, preferring one another, giving each other the benefit of the doubt, etc.

This is because if *agape* love is not in control, then only *human* love remains in control, and human love does not—indeed, *cannot*—last forever. Remember 1 Corinthians 13:4–8 (paraphrased): "*Agape Love endures long and is patient and kind… Agape Love does not insist on its own rights or its own way, for it is not self-seeking… Agape Love does not remember wrongs done against it… Agape Love never gives up on people, never stops trusting, never stops hoping, and never quits. Agape Love never dies…*" Allowing the power of *agape* love to have preeminence in a marriage will make that marriage last "until death does us part."

QUESTIONS:

1. Are you disappointed to finally realize that a spouse is never the cure-all for all your needs? Has marriage lost its luster?
2. In what ways and areas of your married life can you plan and practice self-denial and submission to God so that His love shines through?

PRAYER:

Gracious Father and Source of Eternal Love, we need Your divine graces in our marriages. Teach us how to submit everything into Your hands so that *Your* forgiveness, *Your* endurance and patience, *Your* beautiful attitude and gracious perspective, *Your* self-sacrificing ways, and *Your* divine love take over in every situation! This we ask In Jesus' name, amen.

Lesson 37: Submit Your Sexuality to God

"So then, whether you eat or drink, or whatever you may do, do all for the honor and glory of God."

1 Corinthians 10:31 (AMP)

"Let every detail in your lives—words, actions, whatever—be done in the name of the Master, Jesus, thanking God the Father every step of the way."

Colossians 3:17 (MSG)

There is no way in the world that the current sexual morals and behaviors of millions of today's Christians are approved by God or the Bible:

- According to the 2014 "State of Dating in America" report from ChristianMingle.com, the largest Christian online dating site, only 13 percent of respondents said they would not have sex before marriage. Only 13 percent said that they would move in together *only after* marriage. All of the rest would have sex or move in together for various reasons (i.e., various excuses) before they were married.[o]

- Two-thirds (67 percent) of those who are 18–34 years old do not believe pre-marital sex is *ever* wrong (State of American Theology Study, Lifeway Research, 2014).

---

o. See http://www.stateofdatingreport.com/findings.htm.

- Relevant Magazine reported in 2011 that 80 percent of unmarried Christian young adults have already had sex.[p]

- CovenantEyes.com's "Pornography Statistics: Annual Report 2013" revealed that 50 percent of Christian men and 20 percent of Christian women say they are addicted to pornography.[q] And, unfortunately, these stats are all getting worse every new survey. More recent information from the Conquer Series states that **"68 percent of church-going men** and over **50 percent of pastors** view porn on a regular basis. Of young Christian adults 18–24 years old, 76 percent actively search for porn."[r]

- According to surveys by Proven Men, 35 percent of married Christian men had sex with someone else while married (31 percent for born-again Christian men). Over one-half (56 percent) of men having had one affair will end up having more than three affairs.[s]

- The percentage of people who believe "homosexuality is a sin" continues to drop. Although the majority of Christians still say homosexuality is a sin, surveys show that 27 percent of "born-again, evangelical, or fundamentalist" Christians (i.e., over 1 out of 4) cannot say that it is a sin. Among people who attend religious services at least once a week, 61 percent say homosexuality is a sin, which means that

---

p. See http://www.christianpost.com/news/are-most-single-christians-in-america-having-sex-56680/.

q. See http://www.covenanteyes.com/pornstats/.

r. https://conquerseries.com/15-mind-blowing-statistics-about-pornography-and-the-church/

s. http://www.provenmen.org/2014pornsurvey/christian-porn-stats/#extra-marital.

almost 40 percent think it's okay! And this was in 2013; lots of minds have "evolved" since then.[t]

- About two-thirds of white mainline Protestants (66 percent) now support same-sex marriage, as do a similar share of Catholics (61 percent). Almost 50 percent of young Evangelicals (18–29 years) favor same-sex marriage[u].

- Women identifying themselves as Protestants obtain 37.4 percent of all abortions in the U.S.; Catholic women account for 31.3 percent, Jewish women account for 1.3 percent, and women with no religious affiliation obtain 23.7 percent of all abortions. Eighteen percent of all abortions are performed on women who identify themselves as "born-again/Evangelical" (part of the Protestant category).[v] Also, a recent study reports that 90 percent of women who've had an abortion also had at least three sexual partners, and nearly 83 percent have cohabited at least once. So that means that a sizable portion of the religion-affiliated aborting women, although these reports don't actually say how much, have had at least three or more sexual partners and/or lived with a male without being married to him. In other words, a large portion of these Christian, Catholic, and Jewish women aren't following the sexual purity standards of the Bible at all. Nor, obviously, are the men who got them pregnant![w]

---

t. http://www.christianitytoday.com/gleanings/2013/january/lifeway-fewer-than-2-in-5-americans-say-homosexuality-is.html.

u. Pew Research.

v. http://www.godlikeproductions.com/forum1/message1839399/pg1.

w. See http://www.christianpost.com/news/study-finds-that-90-of-women-whove-had-an-abortion-also-had-at-least-3-sexual-partners-112722/, and for the actual very interesting report, http://downloads.frc.org/EF/EF14A37.pdf.

So obviously, the morality of many Christians today is extremely low and definitely unbiblical in the area of sexuality. People, this is not discipleship. Indeed, this is not biblical Christianity at all! This violates numerous clear scriptural mandates and direct biblical injunctions. It is time for lots of us Christians to quit fooling ourselves about truly knowing God and being in fellowship with Him.

The Bible is very plain regarding human sexuality, from Moses' Seventh Commandment, "*Thou shalt not commit adultery,*" to Paul's New Testament injunction, "Don't let sexual sin, perversion of any kind, or greed even be mentioned among you. This is not appropriate behavior for God's holy people" (Ephesians 5:3, GW). Biblically, sexual behavior of any type is permitted only within God-defined marriage between a male and a female: "Marriage is honorable in every way, so husbands and wives should be faithful to each other. God will judge those who commit sexual sins, especially those who commit adultery" (Hebrews 13:4, GW), and "But in order to avoid sexual sins, each man should have his own wife, and each woman should have her own husband. Husbands and wives should satisfy each other's sexual needs… However, if you cannot control your desires, you should get married. It is better for you to marry than to burn with sexual desire" (1 Corinthians 7:2–3,9, GW).

Additional references are found in Leviticus 20; Numbers 5; Deuteronomy 22 and 27; Romans 1:24–29 and 13:13; 1 Corinthians 5:1, 9–11 and 6:9–20; 2 Corinthians 12:21; Ephesians 4:19–20 and 5:3–5; Colossians 3:5; 1 Thessalonians 4:3; 1 Timothy 1:10; Hebrews 12:16; Revelations 21:8 and 22:15; et. al.

However, no one will ever be able to overcome sexual temptation and live sexually pure, especially in today's sex-saturated society, *without first submitting their sexuality to God.* If He owns you and your life, then He also owns your sexuality, your romantic life, your reproductive rights and capabilities, your relationships, and everything else related to human sexuality. Nothing can be held back from Him. You must recognize and submit to the fact that God made marriage between a male and female as the only proper container and expression of human sexuality. *That* is *His* way, and everything else is some other human-created, flesh-justified way. This fact we Christians must submit to, regardless of how much things have changed and how far standards have fallen in the world.

As this chapter's introductory verses instruct, every detail in a Christian life must be under the Lordship of Jesus Christ, performed in His name, to His honor and glory, and as His representatives. And there is no way in the world that the above sexual behaviors can be performed in His name, to His glory, or as His representatives.

But the stats above and the one following engender the question, Are we even *willing* to submit? The American Bible Society's 2013 "State of the Bible" study conducted by the Barna Group showed that only 17 percent of self-identifying Christian adults say they would "be interested in receiving input and wisdom from the Bible on romance and sexuality."[x]

So, it's obvious that multitudes of Christians do not follow biblical guidelines for their sexuality and do not even *intend* to allow God and the Bible to speak to them concerning such! It's easy to deduce from this that they want to *force a change of God's way instead of accepting it,* and, indeed, they are actually *defying* Him. History clearly shows that nothing good has ever come from blatant defiance against God, especially regarding human sexuality. In his 1956 book, *The American Sex Revolution* (p.6), the eminent

---

x. https://www.christianpost.com/news/americas-bible-hypocrisy-study-shows-disconnect-between-beliefs-and-behavior.html

Harvard sociologist, Pitirim Sorokin, analyzing 5,000 years of human cultures, argued that *"no society has ceased to honor the institution of marriage and survived."* We truly prosper *only* to the degree we submit to Him and to His life-giving principles of life.

QUESTIONS:

1. What is the main principle that determines whether a sexual behavior or practice is biblically approved or not?
2. If you have a problem with sexual purity, what is your plan to overcome it, and when will you start?

PRAYER:

Oh, gracious, forgiving Father, Your divine mercy and grace are what Your people and all people need. Too many of us have strayed away from Your standards of purity, much to our own detriment. Please favor us with enlightenment and conviction so that we will be able to bring our sexuality under Your control. It is for our own good and Your glory we ask this, In Jesus' name. Amen.

Chapter Six
Where Do We Go from Here?

Lesson 38: The Greatest Act of Worship a Christian Can Do

"So here's what I want you to do, God helping you: Take your everyday, ordinary life—your sleeping, eating, going-to-work, and walking-around life—and place it before God as an offering..."
Romans 12:1-2 (The Message)

"That's the most sensible way to serve God."
Romans 12:1 (CEV)

"Considering what he has done, it is only right that you should worship him in this way."
Romans 12:1 (ERV)

If you are a Christian who has spent much of your life living selfishly and doing your own thing, then you need to repent for such rebellion. If you have never made a complete consecration by absolutely surrendering your life and *everything* in it to Him and His control alone, then you need to repent for holding back on God and make that consecration. Or, if you made such a consecration long ago but have since failed to abide by it—that is, you have taken yourself off the altar and refused to be a "living sacrifice"—then, once again, you need to repent and renew that consecration.

You *owe* it to God. *Anything less than absolute surrender and total submission to* His *will is some form of rebellion, no matter what else you may call it or how else you might excuse it.* Remember, the biggest winner in this situation is *you*, not God. You receive unspeakable peace, rest, and freedom, divine protection in all circumstances of life, *and the elimination of all your troubles (because once they are truly submitted into God's hands, they no longer trouble you)*! Absolute surrender is the *only* way to gain this.

Hear the words of one old gospel song by Elisha A Hoffman, "Is Your All on the Altar?":

You have longed for sweet peace, and for faith to increase,
And have earnestly, fervently prayed.
But you cannot have rest, or be perfectly blest
Until all on the altar is laid…

Is your all on the altar of sacrifice laid?
Your heart does the Spirit control?
You can only be blest and have peace and sweet rest
As you yield Him your body and soul.[11]

The fact of the matter is that all of life belongs to God anyway. "In Him we live and move and have our being" (Acts 17:28, KJV). Not one person in the world has asked to be here or has given life to himself or herself. It is not within our control at all but in God's alone. Not even Satan has control of life.

But the moment we arrive here, full of the life that God alone has given, we immediately begin trying to take over our own lives. We spend the rest of our lives trying to control our lives, hoarding them, trying to enhance them, protect them, make them into something super great, and generally seeking to make ourselves immortal and invulnerable. And we do all of this independently of the God who gave us that life in the first place, refusing to allow *even Him* to have any say-so regarding the lives He has so lovingly donated to us!

It would seem that since He gave life, He would know how it ought to be lived. He ought to know how it should be valued, protected, saved, and immortalized. Yet, we generally never seek Him about it. We just live our lives the way we want to live them, ignoring God's will, God's way, and God's Word, hoping that He will somehow approve of what we are doing.

Why? We do this because the very life within us has a way of making us believe that we are almost immortal, strong, in control, able to survive independently of God. Life itself is very deceiving. This is called the "pride of life" (1 John 2:16), i.e., the pride that comes *from* life. The *Amplified* version defines "*the pride of life*" as the "*assurance in one's own resources or in the stability of earthly things.*" It is the spirit of life within us that causes us to revel and exult and glory in our own life as if it is something that we ourselves have made and maintained.

But life is a gift—from God alone. All too often, we never wake up to realize that life, death, and what happens in between are really not in our control after all—until we come face to face with our own mortality and realize how helpless we really are. Then we finally realize that this is God's thing all the way. He alone is sovereign, and we bow our knees and our hearts to Him. He alone is sovereign, but He is also so knowledgeable, so powerful and able, and so wonderfully loving that *we absolutely cannot lose by trusting Him completely*!

The Pride of Life

© 2012 Philip A Matthews
https://www.youtube.com/watch?v=OyV_fmFXAAM
(Buy at https://www.amazon.com/dp/B008PVJA2K/ref=pm_ws_tlw_trk12)

The sky is bright and sunny, the flowers full and fair.
All nature hums in harmony, while birds fly through the air.
Then from the dust of Eden, with His artistic eyes,
God forms a man called "Adam," and
Upon the ground he lies, upon the ground he lies.

Upon the ground still lifeless—A lump of clay so cold,
Till God breathes on him and he then becomes a living soul.
The Spirit motivates him. He jumps up from the clay.
He looks around him at the world,
Then slowly walks away, he slowly walks away.

The man just keeps on walking farther from God astray,
Forgetting that he's nothing but "Sophisticated Clay."
Oh, and God just keeps on watching, until at last He cried:
"I made a man; Man made a mess,
Through selfishness and pride, through selfishness and pride!"

Bridge: The Pride of Life is in control. It mars the mind, deceives the soul.
It fills the world with misery and keeps us all from harmony.

What makes a man start thinking that he's more than worthless soil?
Why can't he see that without God, he cannot live at all?
Let God take back His spirit, the poor man only dies,
A lump of cold clay as before.

Upon the ground he lies, upon the ground he lies.

A king, a prince, a millionaire,
But on the ground he lies, upon the ground he lies.
The biggest bigshot anywhere,
But on the ground he lies, upon the ground he lies.[12]

Knowing this, it should be obvious that the greatest love and worship we can possibly give to our Creator is to yield to Him the complete control of our lives. This is the ultimate worship: to lovingly trust Him with our lives, to breathe every breath in submission to His will and His way, to promise Him that we will never abuse this life He has given us by going outside of His will for anything, to yield our spirits to Him, to accept everything that He allows into our lives, to willingly and gladly submit to the idea that everything we are or ever hope to be is in His control alone. That is true worship—*the greatest act of worship a Christian can do!*

As the Deer

You alone are my Strength, my Shield;
To You alone may my spirit yield.
You alone are my heart's desire,
And I long to worship You.[13]

Or, it can be said through another song:

I Worship You, My God
© 2005 Philip A Matthews

I worship You, my God, with every breath I take.
I worship You, my God, with every move I make.
How could I spend a moment not glorifying You?
In everything I do, I worship You, my God.

My purpose here is only to worship You alone—
A channel of Your wonderful blessings.
My heart is now Your throne.
Your Kingdom and Your glory, my one and only aim.
I bow before You, Jesus, and bless Your holy name…

Or in the words of one more lyricist yet:

We Must Be Holy
By D. S. Warner

Jesus has taken my load of sin, Such love no tongue can tell;
Then should I not resign to Him my life and all my will?

Can I behold the dear Savior's death and yet withhold a part?
Oh, can I draw one selfish breath and not give all my heart?

If everyone in the *church* would do this, the church of God in this world would become so powerful that it would literally "*turn this world upside down*" (Acts 17:6, KJV) in less than one generation! Or, actually, it would turn this world right side up! And if everybody in the *world* would do this, this world would literally be heaven on earth!

QUESTIONS:

1. Why do you think it seems so difficult for Christians to relinquish their death grip on their own lives and learn to live only for the Lord?

PRAYER:

Heavenly Father and Almighty Creator and Redeemer, help us to act like created beings who have absolutely nothing that we did not receive from You. Help us to remember that we belong to You; we are the "sheep of *Your* pasture" (Psalm 100:3) and are not "owners of ourselves" (1 Corinthians 6:19). Help us to renounce the beloved habit of living life and making choices that benefit only ourselves. Help us to recognize—and accept—the fact that we are here on this earth *only* for Your pleasure and Your glory, nothing else (Revelation, 4:11). In the name of our blessed Redeemer, the only truly Beautiful Being to ever walk this earth, Jesus Christ, amen.

Lesson 39: Submission to the Singular Motivation of Christ Alone Unifies the Church

"The goal is for all of them to become one heart and mind—Just as you, Father, are in Me and I in You, So they might be one heart and mind with Us. Then the world might believe that You, in fact, sent Me."

John 17:21 (The Message)

Christians throughout the Body of Christ increasingly recognize that the many walls we Christians have erected to separate us from each other should be torn down. Christian unity is Jesus' standard and desire, but unfortunately, we have lost it, refusing to fellowship each other over doctrines, histories, personalities, traditions, etc. We recognize that the church will never reach its full power, potential, and effectiveness if we continue to allow our differences to prevent us from loving each other despite the many individual brands of Christianity.

Indeed, this is the *only* way the world will ever be reached: *It will take many different groups of Christians having different spheres of influence using different means and methods of outreach to win different cultures and groups of unbelievers to the same Christ.* Let's recognize this as *God's* plan and quit pressuring each other to fit into the same religious mold, then disowning each other when we don't. Division is not merely having differences but not having *love* despite those differences! Division is *refusing* to recognize, love, and accept other true Christians as our brothers and sisters in Christ.

Unity is recognizing our many differences and fully and lovingly accepting and working with each other despite them.

This requires us to make a few comments about Christian motivation. The church of God in the earth is the Body of Christ, consisting of all the blood-washed souls in the world. At the head of that Body is Jesus Christ Himself. Just as in a natural body, the head controls everything that happens in that body, so also in the Body of Christ, the Head controls everything. Every member in that Body, no matter how small and insignificant, must have a direct connection to the Head. *"Christ is the head, and the whole body depends on him"* (Colossians 2:19, ERV). Otherwise, that member ceases to be a viable part of the Body. If the nerve connection is broken or some other malady interferes with the connection, that member is paralyzed and unable to receive communication from the Head. Eventually, that member is cut off and dies (John 15:1–6). But the point is that the power, energy, and motivation from the Head *radiates* throughout the Body into every single member of the Body and then out into the world. Thus, every member is, in some way, an *expression or reflection* of the Head.

The concept of the Head radiating and expressing Himself through every member is a very significant concept. Every member *reflects* something that is going on in the Head. The desires and wishes of the Head, the burden of the Head, the love and grace of the Head, the power and motivation of the Head—these influences should be what radiates down through every member. When every member has the spirit of Christ, the mind of Christ, the burden of Christ, the love of Christ for souls, and the desire of Christ, then unity is possible. But when the singular motivation of Christ is *not* radiating through every Christian, then Christians find themselves unable to practice unity. There are simply too many different motivations.

This is what has happened to the Body of Christ in the world today. Too many Christians are not reflecting the mind and burden of Christ. *The pure, single desire for God alone that Christ possessed is not their chief desire. The love that motivated Christ is not what motivates them. They are not radically submitted and emptied of self. They are driven by some other selfish motivation, a love of themselves.* As Paul wrote to the Philippians: "For the others all seek [to advance] their own interests, not those of Jesus Christ (the Messiah)" (Philippians 2:21, AMP).

For example, one leader is driven by the burden of Christ, but his co-worker is driven by a desire to save his preaching career and/ or his salary or pension. One brother is motivated by the desire to present Christ alone to the world, but another is motivated to present his *brand* of Christianity. One is trying to save souls, but another is trying to save the church or the denomination. One is trying to obey the Great Commission by bringing sinful, un-churched people in, while the other is trying to keep the church "clean" and driving them out because, as one church deacon *preposterously* told me one day, they are of the "wrong element!" Of course, Jesus Himself got in trouble for trying to win folks from the "wrong element" (Luke 15:2). And at one time, we were *all* part of the "wrong element!"

Continuing with our real-world examples, one Christian is trying to build *God's* Kingdom, but another is selfishly building his *own* little kingdom to boost his own ego and make tons of money! Another cannot make an honest move for God and biblical Truth because he is trying to maintain his political clout within some religious movement. Another is driven by the need to maintain approval from a religious group and to keep from offending some-body. Still, another is making all his moves obsessed with the fear of what other Christians might think of him. Some are "working for Christ" to bolster their own egos and boost their own feelings of self-worth, thus really working for themselves. Some have a zeal for Christ, and some have a zeal for the success of their churches. Some have a zeal for themselves. "Though some are preaching Christ out of envy and competition, others do it out of a good heart. One group is motivated by pure love… others from selfish ambition…" (Philippians 1:15–17, BBE/MSG/NASB). And some want Christ to be preached, but, like the carnally motivated disciples in *Mark 9:38–40,* only if "they follow us."

Listen: There is absolutely no way for Christians, within any specific movement or among movements, to work together in unity if they are not all reflecting the true Spirit, love, burden, drive, motivation, and desires of Jesus Christ—and nothing else. It is time for all of us to radically submit our own little personal motivations, ambitions, and agendas under the singular motivation of Jesus Christ alone—the love of God!

The sobering question is, *Who* is going to preach *Christ alone,* without fear and without selfish desires, from an absolutely *pure* motivation? How many Kingdom workers are in this thing *only* because of a love for Christ and *not* because of what they are getting out of it—power, money, prestige, recognition, fulfillment of personal ambitions; personal kingdom-building; feelings of self-worth and accomplishment; emotional sentimentality and longings for the "good old times;" spiritual conscience soothing; maintaining of social or political connections; perpetuation of church identity, history, traditions, and doctrinal preservation; a need to feel busy and important; emotional security; or some other *selfish* reward? *With all this stuff motivating Christian leaders and laypeople alike, unity is utterly impossible! We can never get on the same page if we are not reading out of the same chapter! And, unfortunately, some of us are not even in the same book!*

It should be noted that Satan himself recognizes that there are only two sides in the spirit world—God's and his. As the pressure and persecution against believers increase daily throughout this world, the devil and his agents don't care what brand of Christianity you preach. All they care about is, Are you on their side? And if you aren't, then they are persecuting *all* Christians, even Christian cults, indiscriminately! Meanwhile, we selfishly motivated, self-loving Christians continue to let our differences keep us from helping each other. When will we learn Jesus' secret: "*Whoever is not against us is for us*" (Mark 9:40, KJV)? If we're not on Satan's side, then we're on *God's* side—*together. Let's act like it! Has the blood of Jesus saved you? Do we share in that "one Spirit, one Lord, one God and Father, one faith, one baptism, one hope" (Ephesians 4:4–6 KJV)? Let's love each other even if we don't agree on everything*! Let's submit our own little personal agendas and follow *God's*.

Is it even God's will for His people to be unified through love? The answer is a resounding, *Yes!* Jesus Himself prayed for this just before He left the world in John 17:21 (The Message): "The goal is for all of them to become one heart and mind—Just as You, Father, are in Me and I in You, So they might be one heart and mind with Us. Then the world might believe that You, in fact, sent Me." He said something similar right after the Last Supper, in John 13:34–35 (The Message): "Let me give you a new command: Love one another. In the same way, I loved you, you love one another. This is how everyone will recognize that you are My disciples—when they see the love you have for each other."

So our disunity, lack of love, and failure to radically submit our motivations under Christ are hindering us from proving that our Lord Jesus Christ is indeed sent from the One True God of Heaven and that we ourselves are indeed His true disciples. In a world as wicked and perverse as ours, is *this* what we want to continue doing? Is this disunity what we want the world to continue seeing? Shouldn't we be working on changing this *ASAP*?

From "Let's Come Together" by Kevin Levar
https://www.youtube.com/watch?v=7Cfw3CbaX-s

...If we come together so many souls will be saved
If we come together so many souls will be changed
If we come together so many bound will be free, They'll be free
We got to come together... I need you, you need me, We're all a part of God's family
So let's not fight, Let's not fuss, Let's worship Jesus... We got to come together...
Let the walls fall down that divide Your body...

QUESTIONS:

1. How do you propose solving the problem of a lack of unity within the Body of Christ in this world? Or do you believe unity among God's people is even possible?
2. What can you do *personally* to help achieve more unity in the Church?

PRAYER:

Lord Jesus, I realize this is a big problem in the Church, the inability of your people to love and accept each other and work together. Help us come together, someway, somehow, at some time. Perhaps it may be by fire and persecution. Whatever You choose to do, feel free, so that Your will may be done in earth as it is in heaven, and so that we may prove that You sent Jesus and we ourselves are His disciples. We pray this, just as He Himself prayed, In Jesus' name. Amen.

Lesson 40: Churches Must Teach and Train Radical Submission

"Jesus, undeterred, went right ahead and gave his charge: 'God authorized and commanded me to commission you: Go out and train everyone you meet, far and near, in this way of life, marking them by baptism in the threefold name: Father, Son, and Holy Spirit. Then instruct them in the practice of all I have commanded you. I'll be with you as you do this, day after day after day, right up to the end of the age.'"

Matthew 28:18–20 (The Message)

The message of the Gospel is that Jesus Christ saves sinners *from* a life of sin and all of its evil consequences and translates them *into* a life of holiness and all of its great benefits. Sin produces victims of evil as a natural consequence. "The wages of sin is death," and not just after this life is over. "He that sows to the flesh shall of the flesh reap corruption" (Galatians 6:8, KJV), now and in the hereafter. But holiness produces blessedness as a natural consequence. "Godliness with contentment is great gain" (1 Timothy 6:6, KJV).

Therefore, Christian churches must begin to emphasize not mere forgiveness of sins and great positive feelings but holiness in practical life. Jesus never limited the Great Commission to just "Go and preach," but His ultimate charge was to "Make disciples… Teach them to obey everything I have told you to do" (Matthew 28:20, ERV). His ultimate goal and desire are for believers to be *disciples* under submission to God. His desire and the crying need of today are for everyone in the church—indeed, the world—to be brought under subjection to the will and way of Christ.

A disciple, a follower, is by definition one who *practices* submission to the will and doctrine of another. One cannot be a disciple and keep doing his or her own thing. *The only true disciple of Christ is one who has given Him complete control of his life in every area so that what comes out for the world to see is Jesus manifesting Himself through that disciple!* To have areas of one's life that Christ does not control prevents that person from being a true follower of Christ and from receiving many of the benefits He has for them.

So rather than concentrating on bringing multitudes of un-converted, still-rebellious, self-seeking people into the church and trying to please and appease them, churches should start concentrating on finding truly honest-hearted people who are willing to fully submit to God in every area of their lives—no more trying to lure people into the church and keep them there with the great music program, the wonderful kids' ministry, or the multi-million-dollar church facility with all its coffee shops and aerobics programs. *Disciples are made by radical submission to God in love, not by bribery, entertainment, or anesthetizing themselves through constant religious distractions.*

The first suggestion is for every local church to start more aggressively teaching people the Word and how to apply its demands to our lives. Better still, get every member into active discipleship programs within the church to enable it to actually "make disciples." Such programs would not be merely educational but actual training, having definite biblical standards of behavior, built-in accountability, required obedience, and scriptural church discipline. Christians should be trained how to hear, know, and follow the voice of the Holy Spirit while they are being taught the eternal principles of the Word.

It is time for every church to take the radical (but biblical) stand that nobody should be allowed to be in a leadership position or an integral part of that ministry if that person is not a true disciple of Christ, daily practicing a life of radical submission to God and

His Word. When this is done in a balanced way according to the instructions in the New Testament, it is not, as many will probably charge, legalism. It is actually the way the church is supposed to operate, by giving the Word and Spirit their proper positions in the church.

Another suggestion is to open Christian discipleship homes for men and women who are ready to experience a total and radical change in their lives. In today's post-modern world, where the pervading lack of moral absolutes has seemingly caused the masses to lose all idea of right and wrong, discipleship homes would allow converts to undergo "24/7" immersion in the Christian faith. This is not a cultic concept but the actual biblical method to teach true Bible-based, Christ-centric living. Jesus Himself used this method with His disciples. It was based on relationship, and they *lived* with Him. Later, the new converts of the apostles' day "*continued steadfastly in the apostles' doctrine,*" "*all who believed were together,*" they were "*daily in the temple,*" and they "*had all things in common*" (Acts 2:42–47, KJV). Today's "go to church on Sunday only" model of Christianity is no longer an effective, world-changing method. Indeed, it has *never* been effective: After 2,000 years, we *still* have managed to save only one-fourth of the world, and most of them are "cultural" Christians, many not knowing Jesus Christ at all.

So, any new Christians entering these homes should be told *up front* that true Christianity *requires* complete submission to God and does not permit half-heartedness, straddling the fence, selfish indulgence, justifying sin, or reserving certain areas of one's life from God's control. This is the method Jesus Himself used with the rich, young ruler who came to Him asking what good thing he could do to obtain eternal life: "*Go and sell everything you own, give it to the poor, and come follow Me*" (Matthew 19:21, KJV).

Jesus barely knew the man, but He let him know the cost of discipleship up front. He used a no-nonsense, no coddling approach.

After that, the task of the discipleship homes would be to concentrate on making those participants the most spiritually sound, holiness-practicing disciples around. Help them to experience first-hand the life-revolutionizing love of God. Teach them how to bring every aspect of their lives into the "obedience of Christ" (2 Corinthians 10:5)—their plans, their purpose for living, their desires, their careers, their relationships, their parenting or marital responsibilities, their sexuality, their daily activities—*everything.*

Teach them to forsake sin completely and to deny self consistently, and make them accountable to a mentor. Help them to acquire a Christ-like character. Teach them humility and modesty in attitude, action, and appearance. Teach them that service to God and ministry to others is the greatest calling in life. Give them a totally biblical worldview. Teach them to know, be sensitive to, and follow the Spirit, but also to know and obey the Word. Require participants to go through inner healing regularly because, in our broken world, everybody carries numerous wounds, insecurities, and other symptoms of brokenness. These are the wounds and weaknesses that prevent us from living like Christ.

Such ministries have great potential to be very fruitful and rewarding because the need is extremely great. Very few people, Christian or otherwise, really know how to bring their lives into complete conformity with the Word of God, and relatively few churches are teaching them anything about it. Discipleship, sanctification, inner healing, holiness—these are not the most practiced or well-loved concepts in the world or the church.

But they are our *only* chance for real transformation—individually or collectively. Eugene Peterson, author of *The Message*

Bible translation, sums it up well in a much-earlier work when he says, *"Millions of people in our culture make decisions for Christ, but there is a dreadful attrition rate. Many claim to have been born again, but the evidence for mature Christian discipleship is slim... There is a great market for religious experience in our world; there is little enthusiasm for the patient acquisition of virtue, little inclination to sign up for a long apprenticeship in what earlier generations of Christians called holiness."[14]*

Therefore, whoever wants to operate such discipleship ministries should be very well aware that probably fewer than one out of ten people who say they want to change their lives is really willing to learn submission to God. Most will merely want God's blessings and continual divine bailouts from the devastation their selfish decisions get them into.

However, for that small, honest ten percent, it is well worth the effort because they will be true, sanctified disciples of Christ. They will love God alone. And they will be the servants God uses to change communities, churches, families, and entire societies.

Discipleship, sanctification, inner healing, practical holiness—these are the areas that the Christian church should take as its emphasis for today. When it does, both the church and the world will be absolutely amazed at the results of the awesome, life-changing power of *Radical Submission to God!*

QUESTIONS:

1. What other methods can you think of to achieve true discipleship in the church?

PRAYER:

O God, when we think of the Great Commission, we realize that you told us to "make disciples," people who not only claim to believe in You but who give up their own lives to allow You to live *Your* life in and through them. Lord, we acknowledge that in many ways, we have completely failed at this most important task, instead creating lots of "Christians" and "decisions for Christ" but very few disciples. Forgive us, and help us first to become true disciples ourselves, then to focus our attention and efforts on making others into true disciples. Help Your Church to realize that the measure of our success is not in how many "decisions" we rustle up but in how many disciples we make. Help us to remember that discipleship begins—and ends—with Radical Submission to God. In the loving name of Jesus, amen.

ENDNOTES

1. Philip A. Matthews, "A Little Part Of His Plan." From the album, I'll Keep Holding On To Jesus, Gospel Harmonizers, ©℗ 1980. https://www.youtube.com/watch?v=9jwzt8icoq8.

2. Fanny J. Crosby, "Blessed Assurance." Great Hymns of the Faith, Singspiration (Zondervan: Grand Rapids, MI, 1968, p. 255).

3. Philip A. Matthews, "He's Everything That I Need." From the album, I'll Keep Holding On To Jesus, Gospel Harmonizers, ©℗ 1980. https://www.amazon.com/dp/B00DU5BB3W/ref=dm_ws_tlw_trk10

4. George Barna, "Born Again Christians Just As Likely to Divorce As Are Non-Christians," Barna Research Online, September 8, 2004, https://www.barna.org/component/content/article/5-barna-update/45-barna-update-sp-657/194-born-again-christians-just-as-likely-to-divorce-as-are-non-christians#.VsJIRhYUXIU. And https://www.barna.org/component/content/article/5-barna-update/45-barna-update-sp-657/56-born-again-adults-less-likely-to-co-habit-just-as-likely-to-divorce#.VsJLCRYUXIU.

5. George Barna, "American Worldview Inventory 2020—At a Glance," Cultural Research center at Arizona Christian University, March 2020. www.barna.org.

6. George Barna, "A Biblical Worldview Has a Radical Effect on a Person's Life," Barna Research Online, December 1, 2003, p.2. www.barna.org.

7. George Barna, "Only Half of Protestant Pastors Have A Biblical Worldview," Barna Research Online, January 12, 2004, p.1. www.barna.org.

8. George Barna, "A Biblical Worldview Has a Radical Effect on a Person's Life," Barna Research Online, December 1, 2003, p.2. www.barna.org.

9. Franklin Wilder, Immortal Mother, (Vantage Press: New York, 1966, p.45).

10. Lecrae Moore, Chris Lee Cobbs, John Williams, "Boasting," as recorded by Lecrae on Rehab (Reach Records, LLC, 2010).

11. Elisha A. Hoffman, "Is Your All On the Altar?" Great Hymns of the Faith, Singspiration (Zondervan: Grand Rapids, MI, 1968), p. 381.

12. Philip A. Matthews, "The Pride of Life." From the album, Original Worship, The Matthews Family © ℗ 2012. https://www.amazon.com/dp/B008PVJA2K/ref=pm_ws_tlw_trk12.

13. Martin Nystrom, "As the Deer." Celebration Hymnal: Songs and Hymns For Worship, Word Music/Integrity Music, p. 548.

14. Eugene H. Peterson, A Long Obedience in the Same Direction: Discipleship In An Instant Society, (InterVarsity Press: Downers Grove, IL, 1980, p. 12).

For further information:
Philip A Matthews
Christian Challenge Ministries
1752 East Avenue J, Suite 186
Lancaster, California 93535
cchallenge@sbcglobal.net
www.christianchallengeministries.org
310-347-1189